MW00874919

CINDY ROBINSON

Bright Girl, Lacks Focus

A Neurodivergent Memoir

Copyright © 2023 by Cindy Robinson

All rights reserved. No part of this publication may be reproduced, stored or transmitted in any form or by any means, electronic, mechanical, photocopying, recording, scanning, or otherwise without written permission from the publisher. It is illegal to copy this book, post it to a website, or distribute it by any other means without permission.

First edition

This book was professionally typeset on Reedsy.
Find out more at reedsy.com

This book is dedicated to all the wildflowers and the ones who know a wildflower when they have one. I am most grateful for the wildflower I gave birth to, and his father who never once tried to stop him (or me) from blossoming.

Foreword

I've read a lot of memoirs and they have been instrumental in my growth as a human. *The Choice* by Edith Eger opened my eyes to the role shame plays in preventing us from seeing ourselves in our true light. She blamed herself for her mother's death in a concentration camp during the Holocaust. She taught me how to blame the Nazi's.

Stephanie Foo taught me about recovering from Complex-PTSD in *What My Bones Know*. Flea, oh my precious Flea (yes, the bassist from The Red Hot Chili Peppers) gifted me with the most beautiful memoir, *Acid for the Children,* perhaps my favorite of them all. He taught me how to fly in the cosmos of my weirdness and he was there waiting for me when I arrived. *Untamed* by Glennon Doyle, a memoir I really didn't enjoy at all, taught me to not try to be the hero in my stories, a mistake I would have undoubtedly made had I not read that book. Tara Westover set me free from shame about my Southern upbringing in *Educated.* Jeannette McCurdy let me know it was ok if I related a little too much to *I'm Glad My Mom Died. Eat, Pray, Love* by Elizabeth Gilbert may have mistakenly made me believe healing was only possible in an Indonesian temple, but at least she made me feel as if healing was possible at all.

I'm a fan of memoirs who is writing a memoir. The prospect of that is overwhelming. There is so much I will likely do wrong and my bar for memoirs is so high. The likelihood for frustration that exists between those two truths is immense. But I move forward anyway, just as I'm sure all of the authors who transformed my life had to do at some point. The messiest and least perfect memoirs are by far my favorites, that is the only thing that brings me solace. Because if I can do anything well, it's messiness and imperfection.

I wanted to use this introduction as an opportunity to answer a question I have every single time I sit down to read a memoir:

How close to the truth is this book?

My answer: As close as I could get it. At the very least, it is a truthful representation of my perspective. Of course, I don't remember exactly what was said in conversations that took place when I was five. But I remember how they were remembered and how they've shaped me over the years, and I've tried to stay very true to that process. I barely consulted with anyone about the accuracy of my memories, for good reason. It is my memoir, afterall. Not my friends' or my loved ones' memoir. But everything I say happened, did happen. This is not another *A Million Little Pieces.*

Now I would like to answer a question that I *never* have when I sit down to read a memoir (but has been nagging in the back of my mind ever since I wrote the first word, so I have to get it out):

Who do I think I am?

My answer: No one. And everyone. I didn't write this memoir because I thought my story was so special. In fact, I wrote it because I think I'm so unspecial. I think a lot of women have lived a life like mine. It's funny how I feel such a deep need to clarify that. When I'm reading memoirs one thing I never do is doubt whether the author had a right to tell their story. I may critique the writing, not identify with the voice, or doubt the author's sincerity, but I've never once doubted their worthiness. I felt compelled to write this book for me, first and foremost. But I felt compelled to publish it for people like me. I want them to feel seen. I want to find them with my words and say hello. The only way to do that is by sucking it up and writing the damn story.

Preface

I was sitting on my couch, sobbing, trying to articulate what I was feeling to my very patient boyfriend, sometime in early 2002. I was 19 years old.

I was not just sitting on any couch, I was sitting on the worst couch ever. A couch a landlord would select for his furnished apartments in Barnesville, Georgia, a town that only had two things: a community college and one of the state's largest prisons.

The fabric color was a mixture of diarrhea brown and dishwater brown. I'm sure the landlord thought it would "go with anything" which was just a nice way of saying it was void of any personality at all. The material was a hybrid between burlap and plastic. It was clear in the making of that couch the two main priorities were durability and stain resistance. Missing from the list of priorities was comfort. It was the itchiest, ugliest, most uncomfortable, shittiest couch on the planet.

I'm able to go into excruciating detail because I spent a lot of time there. I woke up on it every morning, a latticed imprint of the fabric on my face and a blaring infomercial in my ear. It was from that couch that I would try my best to pump myself up to go to class, but never did. After I gave up attempting to go to class, I'd fall back to sleep on that couch until well into the afternoon. Then, when I woke up a 2nd time around noon, I'd watch daytime TV from it.

Daytime TV shows were for pathetic people. You could tell because all of the commercials were for personal injury lawyers and career training schools. They knew if you were home in the middle of the day, and unbusy enough to be watching TV, you should probably be thinking about how you're going to make some money soon. It appeared my two best options were to become a nail technician or file a personal injury claim.

I also sat on that couch for all of my meals. Most of which consisted of Lean Cuisine microwavable dinners or fast food restaurants. Once I had my fill of Dunkin Donut holes and McDonald's Happy Meals, somewhere around 2am, I fell back asleep to the sound of the TV on that couch. The TV was on 24/7 in that apartment. Silence summoned the mind-demons and Forensic Files was the only thing that could keep them at bay.

And now, as was a regular occurance, I was crying on that same, shitty couch. I was a soon-to-be thrice college dropout. This 3rd attempt at college was, in my mind, my last attempt to see if I had any hope of becoming a real adult. It wasn't going well. Forget college, I couldn't even remember to buy basic necessities for myself, like toilet paper. When I ran out (which was all the time), I would have to use napkins from the aforementioned fast food restaurants, then I would resort to paper towels, and - as a final act of desperation - actual towels. The majority of the time, my all-brown furnished apartment smelled like old McDonald's bags and sour milk from bowls of cereal that were left out on the counter for days. It was so bad, the landlord once came by to check on the apartment and was so disgusted he gave me a 30-day eviction notice. However, depressing as all of that was, none of those things were the reason I was crying that day.

With my head in my hands and snot/tears seeping through my fingers, I said "I just feel like I am destined for more than this. I hate school, I hate work... and I feel like I'll be doing both forever! I think I'm meant for so much more!"

My boyfriend softly took my snot-soaked hand. "So what *are* you passionate about?" he said. "What *do* you want to do?"

I paused for a second to muster the courage to say what had been creeping into my mind for the last several days. "I want to be a writer!" I bursted into tears the moment I said it.

"Ok..." he said with a surface-level gentility that was clearly masking an abundance of caution. His long pause was likely allowing time for him to gather his thoughts, of which I'm sure there were plenty. Thoughts like: *Are you insane? What do you have to write about? You can't even commit to doing the dishes, much less commit to writing a book! How are you planning to pay your rent while you're making zero dollars writing because no publisher is looking for a nineteen year old college flunkie who lives in a shitty furnished apartment that is mostly paid for by disability money for your clearly unmanaged ADHD...*

But he didn't say any of those things (out loud anyway). Instead, he said, "Do you have much experience with writing?"

He already knew the answer to that question, of course I didn't. In high school my Language Arts teachers all found me unremarkable. They commented more on my excessive talking than my writing. I thought all of their classes were boring and pointless. I hadn't shown up to a Literature class in college long enough to learn anything. Aside from the several half-written, poorly-told stories I wrote as a child, I had absolutely no notable experience or talent at writing anything of any kind.

"I know it sounds crazy!" I plummeted my head into my hands once again. "I don't know why that feels like my destiny but it just *does!*" The more I talked, the more insane I sounded, and I knew it. But I couldn't stop the words from tumbling out of my mouth. And I was not about to admit I was doubting my sanity to my boyfriend. I needed to keep a united front that referring to "my destiny" was a sign of otherworldly wisdom and definitely not a sign of mental instability.

"Ok, if that's what you feel then why don't you change your major to Journalism?" he suggested. Oh, bless his heart with his logical, practical solutions.

"*No!* I feel like I could write better if I could just start writing, but I can't do all the school required to be a writer! I just *can't*! Why do there have to be so many steps to doing anything?! Why can't I just *write*?! You don't believe in me at all I can tell!" My tears boiled into anger. I looked for where to place the cause of the anger, as I was not an option. It could only fall on the only other person in the room. My face ran hot and I was now angry at *him*. I thought his logical solution was somehow insensitive to my personal awakening. I stormed out of the room and into my filthy bathroom and slammed the door. I bashed a few things around just to let him know how upset and hurt I was by his reasonable suggestion. I collapsed on the floor and sobbed, making sure I was loud enough so he could hear. Then, after realizing he wasn't rushing to my aid to apologize, I wiped my tears and sat in silence. Sniffling and suffocated by the silence, I twirled the frayed edges of my bath towel that was lying on the floor and wondered what it felt like to not be like this. I wished my life was completely different. I wished I was completely different.

* * *

As I sat down to write this book, I had the same feeling I had trouble articulating back then. It's the same feeling I've had every time I write anything - from an article to a caption on Instagram. It is a gnawing feeling from within, that words are fighting their way out, but I don't know if I'm worthy enough to say them. They ache and pull at me and beg me to put them on paper, but they give no context or promise as to why. I fear they have not taken into consideration my inadequacies or the embarrassment that is to follow after I share them. They demand to be written either way and give zero fucks about the consequences.

This book is to honor that disastrous, hard-to-love girl sitting on her disgusting bathroom floor, wishing her life was completely different. The one who lashed out at the people who loved her most because she didn't know how to accept their love. The one who first felt that ache to write but had no idea it would take more than 20 years to be ready to become a writer. I am grateful for her Intuition and how relentlessly she protected it, even as she questioned it herself.

A special thank you to the bottomless-patience boyfriend, Brad, who didn't walk away that day or any day since. He is now my husband and still makes frustratingly practical suggestions to my always-existential problems.

I

BREAKING THE GIRL

1

EARLIEST MEMORY

I have to admit my earliest memory wasn't the best. I have tried hard to remember something - anything - before it. At first, I hoped that my first memory was in Kindergarten, when I drew pants on a T-Rex coloring page in class. My teacher, Mrs. Upchurch (whom I not-so-affectionately referred to as Mrs. Up-chuck) got upset with me and said I wasn't taking the assignment seriously. Because, after all, six-year-olds should be, above all other things, serious. It really stressed me out that she thought I was making a mockery of her assignment - I just thought it was funny.

Daddy picked me up from school once a week on Tuesdays. That was the custody arrangement between him and Mama when they got divorced. It just so happened the "T-Rex Pants" incident fell on a day he picked me up.

"Mr. Garrett, today during a coloring assignment Cindy failed to follow the rules. She had specific instructions to color the dinosaur green, and she put brown pants on him. This distracted several of the students and got many of them off-track. So I told her I was going to share this with you and you may not be very happy to hear it," Mrs. Up-chuck said with a smug look on her face, the perfect role model for old school marms everywhere. I looked at the ground and didn't utter a word.

"Oh, thank you for letting me know, Mrs. Upchurch. I'll talk to her about it on the way home." Daddy spoke in a soft, serious voice that reassured her he was dedicated to his child's education above all other things, including fun. We gathered my tiny backpack and left. Things were silent for a bit in the car. I knew I was mad but I was sorting out who exactly I was mad at and why. Mrs. Up-chuck was a real bitch, but Daddy seemed to agree with her. Or maybe I was mad at myself for not being able to follow simple instructions.

He interrupted my thoughts with, "Don't listen to Mrs. Upchurch." For the first time since she tattled on me I looked up. "She sounds like she has a stick up her butt. I think it's cool you drew pants on a dinosaur. Who's to say dinosaurs didn't wear pants? They were all dead by the time we got here." I was smiling really big now.

Yeah, I thought, *Mrs. Up-chuck has a stick up her butt.* The image not only made me giggle, it made me feel a lot better that he didn't agree with that old wench. Plus it felt nice to know putting pants on a T-Rex wasn't the end of my academic career.

"I bet she poops sticks out every day." I giggled. He returned my laughter, which I loved, so I doubled down. "I call her Mrs. Up-chuck because her face looks like vomit!" I loudly mimicked vomit erupting from my mouth and fake smeared it all over my face.

"Ok, ok. That's enough." he said. I admit it was a bit much. I never quite knew when to let a joke go. The car was silent again, but this time the silence felt a little better. "Up-chuck is pretty clever, though," he said, a little accidental chuckle slipping out at the end. "Just don't call her that at school." My big smile returned.

That would have been a nice first memory. But T-Rex Pants happened in elementary school and I knew my earliest memory was from before

I started school.

There was another contender I had hoped to be my earliest memory: the time I predicted a tornado. I remember walking outside and feeling a distinct pressure in the air. The sky was grey, but not a normal grey. An eerie, creepy, greenish-grey. I saw trash blowing across the street in a particular type of wind I hadn't felt before. The entire situation was curious, and I thought, *It feels like a tornado is coming.*

Lo and behold, later that day we were tucked into our basement with a radio, waiting out a tornado warning. Everyone else was concerned with our safety, but I was utterly amazed with myself. *My God, I have the ability to predict tornadoes!* I thought proudly.

Maybe it wasn't a total superpower. Perhaps it was the fact that I overheard several teachers expressing frustration that they didn't do early dismissal due to possible tornadoes. Or maybe the weatherman predicting tornadoes on the radio on the way to school was a clue. But I decided to go with, *I have a tornado-predicting superpower.*

But, alas, cool as that moment was for me at the time, that was not my earliest memory. That story involved teachers and rides to school and, like I said before, my earliest memory happened before I started school.

There's no delicate way to put this so I'll rip the bandage right off: my earliest memory is of being molested.

Mama, who had been divorced from Daddy since I was two, remarried a man named Larry a year after their divorce. He had a son, Jesse, who was seven years older than me and my new stepbrother. Everything was cool with Jesse (I'm assuming) until one day when I was around four. He entered puberty and our relationship changed.

I don't remember what our dynamic was like before the abuse started. All I have is my memory of our relationship changing and wishing that it hadn't changed in that way. He treated me like I was special during

5

the daytime. And I somehow knew that the only reason he treated me special was because of what happened at night.

Every other weekend when he visited I could feel my heart flutter with excitement and like something was wrapped around my throat at the same time. It's strange to feel both dread and elation at the sight of someone (though this wouldn't be the last person who made me feel this way). One day, about a year and a half after the abuse began, it came to an abrupt halt.

"Girls?" Mama shouted from downstairs.

"Yeah!" we echoed back in unison.

"Can you come down here?"

"Why?" again, in unison.

"We need to have *talk time*."

Talk Time was a term Mama had coined for any time she needed to have a serious talk with us. Almost always, these talks were much more unpleasant than they were pleasant. They were usually about things we had been doing wrong or ways we had been hurting her feelings lately. She always marketed them as open discussions where we could connect with one another and say anything, but they invariably ended in a lecture and a sick feeling in the pit of my stomach. Regardless of how much we hated them, we knew it was not an option to decline one. Pal (my older sister) and I marched downstairs into my room and sat on my bed.

"What is *this* about?" Mama revealed a stack of papers with the letters *DIKSHUNARY* scribbled across the top. I always confused the word "diary" with "dictionary".

Oh no, I thought, *I'm so stupid. Why didn't I write diary? If I had written diary she would have known it was private and left it alone. But since I'm so stupid and wrote dictionary, now I'm going to be in so much trouble.* My stomach collapsed in on itself. I didn't say a word. She looked right at me.

"Cindy? Did you write this?" Her finger pointed directly to the line where I had written *Jesse pulls down my pantees and lays on top of me at nite.* On the line below I had written *Dinosaurs are my favrit* and right above it was *Grandad is borink and talks to mutch.* There wasn't any chance of denying I wrote it, either, as Pal was six years older than me and had impeccable penmanship. This thing was full of spelling errors, my signature. I just shrugged my shoulders. This was my deepest, darkest secret. No words would come out even if I wanted them to.

"Does this really happen?! Answer me!" Her voice sounded like the sparks that shoot off of a crackling fire and burn your arm. I could feel anger. I assumed that anger was directed at me. I was, after all, the one who did the bad thing with Jesse. The room stayed silent. She looked at Pal.

"Do you know anything about this? Does Jesse do this with you too?!"

Pal's eyes widened and she quickly shook her head no. This wasn't news to me. I already knew her answer was no. Because one day, not too long before this interrogation, I built up the courage to ask her if the nighttime thing happened to her too. To be exact, I busted in the bathroom while she was on the toilet and blurted out, "Does Jesse pull your panties down too?". I was never known for my good timing or tactfulness.

Likely distracted by my violation of her privacy, she replied, "What?! No!", followed by, "What are you talking about?!", and ending with, "Get out of the bathroom!". I ran out, shut the door, and we never talked about it again.

She was only eleven or twelve years old, she wasn't equipped to know how to respond to a question like that, much less while on the toilet. She was a kid. She was a safe person for me or I would have never even mentioned it to her in the first place. But I will admit, I was disappointed to realize I was the only one. It made me feel even more like it was my fault, like I did something to cause it. She somehow knew how to make that not happen to her but, whatever that was, I didn't know how to do it.

So I already knew I was the only one. But Pal and I both knew we should keep that story to ourselves.

"Ok… It's going to be ok." Mama said, as much to herself as to us. She took one of our hands in each of hers. "I have already talked with Larry and you will never have to see Jesse again. We're not going to let him come near you girls until he gets some help."

There was that mixed feeling again. Of both relief and devastation. I was sad I would never see the cool-ass boy who could get further than anyone in Mario Bros., taught me about Beastie Boys, and loved blowing up fire ant beds with firecrackers. But I was also relieved to be able to sleep in my bed all night every night without having to roll over on my stomach, pull my panties down, and allow him to lie on top of and touch me wherever he wanted. Pal and I still hadn't said a word. We both just started crying.

"Now girls, I need to tell you something else and it's very serious. You have to listen to me." We both looked up at her like, *Jesus Christ, there's more?!* She took a deep breath. "You cannot tell your father about this. I'm serious. If you tell him the police will come take you away from me and you'll never see me again."

Mama was speaking to both of us but looking directly at Pal and I knew why. I'm pretty easy to keep quiet… clearly. I had just kept a pretty big secret from my whole family for the last 18 months, which probably would have been a lot longer if a clerical error hadn't ratted me out. But Pal wasn't so easily silenced. She and Daddy were besties. They had been since the day she was born. Plus Pal was not threatened by never seeing Mama again, it may have felt more like a promise. She and Mama were never compatible with one another. But, lucky for Mama, this was a promise she wanted to keep. She couldn't imagine

8

telling this to Daddy.

I've wished so much to be able to conjure just one earlier memory, one that didn't involve abuse. I desperately wanted to know what it felt like to have a "before" time in my life when I was innocent, and not have every single moment of my life tainted by darkness.

That's the funny thing about memories. I learned once that people aren't supposed to remember before age seven. Long-term memories attach to emotion, that's how they're made. That's why most people don't remember before age seven, because their emotions just aren't complex enough for the memory to have anything to attach to. The exceptions to that rule are traumatic memories. Because of their intensity, they have something for the memory to attach to. Which is why I can vividly remember the nighttime thing with Jesse... because it was traumatic.

2

SHOW ME YOUR WEIRD

In elementary school I had a best friend named Beth Daniel. I rode home after school with her every day. We spent most of our time together outside. We would walk down to the stream behind her house and find tadpoles or, on a really good day, salamanders. Technically, the stream was not on her property. But in South Georgia in the early 90s, if you owned a lot of land you expected there to be random children playing on it at any given moment, especially if it had a body of water. That was just obvious.

When we weren't trespassing, we would jump on the trampoline and dare each other to say cuss words. Neither one of us ever had the courage to do it. The closest we ever got was the first two letters: "Daaaa-" or "Shhhhh-". We would also spend a lot of time either torturing or avoiding her little sister, Julie. She was one year younger, which was the equivalent of a baby in our eyes. Julie always tried to call Beth out for acting differently around me.

"Why don't we play family like me and you did yesterday?" she'd say. Or "You love Strawberry Shortcake! You asked me to play with them last week!". Beth would deny all accusations of baby lame-ness. I knew Julie was telling the truth, but I also knew how desperate playtime could get when you didn't have anyone your own age to play with, so I pretended to believe Beth when she denied Julie's claims.

On very special occasions Beth and I would get to play our favorite game: Dead Animals. Dead Animals was when we would find roadkill or other dead animals (hence the name) while outside exploring. First, we would mourn the loss of these poor street victims (since Beth lived off of a busy highway, most of the animals lost their lives at the hands of a speeding vehicle). We would organize a funeral or perform a ritual to release their souls. Then, once the souls were free, we would investigate the cause of death on their bodies like forensic scientists. With sharpened sticks as scalpels and not a drop of hand sanitizer in sight, we would dig into these poor creatures as best we could to see how they may have died. Though the fact that the crime scene was in the middle of the road, and their mid-section was completely flattened, should have been all the evidence we needed. After the autopsy, the show would begin. We would become marionettes by using sticks to scoop up their bodies and perform the most lurid puppet show that would make P.T. Barnum a little queasy.

* * *

A Macabre Performance of the Utmost Classiness

LADY DIGGERY (a flattened squirrel): Oh my, Mr. Diggery, the country is so different from the city. There is dirt everywhere. However will I keep my pristine white dresses clean?

MR. DIGGERY (the half-eaten frog): My lovely Mrs. Diggery, I will buy you new dresses each time one is dirtied. For I have enough money to buy you all the dresses in the county!

11

MR. KRATCHITY (an opossum, always in abundant supply): Mr. Diggery, may we speak privately?

MR. KRATCHITY AND MR. DIGGERY WALK TO THE SIDE AND LEAN IN FOR A PRIVATE CONVERSATION.

MR. KRATCHITY: *(whispers)* I think Lady Diggery is a gold digger. She's just using you for your money, sir. I'm worried that woman is going to drain your oil money dry!

MR. DIGGERY: Nonsense! She is the love of my life. How dare you question her loyalty! Do that again and you're out on your keester!

MR. KRATCHITY: Yes, sir. I'm sorry, sir.

* * *

We had so much fun with our performances. Our dramas were dramatic, our stomachs like iron, and our audience was only ourselves. One of the coolest discoveries we ever made was a severed deer torso (complete with antlers and one dangling leg) who required both of us to operate properly. One person held the head by the antlers and the other operated the barely attached front leg that dangled from the torso.

3

PAL

"This should be your theme song!"

New Attitude by Patti LaBelle was playing on the car radio. Mama turned the volume up to an unbearable level. She and Pal were in yet another argument. They were never close, but now that my sister was thirteen it seemed like Mama had a personal vendetta against her.

"Because you need a *New Attituuuude!*" Mama sang in an increasingly obnoxious voice. It was the stage of their argument where Mama used cruelty to try and break Pal's spirit while Pal acted like she didn't care about anything in the whole wide world. I sat in the backseat and wondered who was going to break first.

Mama sang the title of the song at the top of her lungs one more time and turned it up a little more.

Pal is six years older than me. I never knew a life without her. We have always had each other to compare notes with during our childhood, which came in handy more times than I can count. Without her, I'm not sure I would have made it to adulthood alive. I dread the reality that she could die before me, and I would be left for the first time ever to navigate my life alone without her notes.

Her real name is Sheri, but I call her Pal. This started when we were making fun of how siblings have cheesy nicknames for each other, like "Sissy" or "Bubba". So we started sarcastically calling one another Pal and never stopped. I guess there was something about having a dumb sibling nickname that we were secretly jealous of.

Pal sat silently in the car the entire ride home, appearing completely unaffected. I was frozen, trying to think of ways to turn the tides on the direction of the argument but each time coming up empty handed.

"Why don't we get some Little Caesar's on the way home?" I asked, hoping somehow cardboard that passes itself off as pizza would bring them together.

"I don't think so. Not with the attitude I've been dealing with all day." Mama responded.

We arrived home and I hoped the space would allow the argument to diffuse as it so often did. Pal would go to her room, I would entertain/distract Mama and cheer her up, and later that evening everyone would reconvene at the dinner table and act like nothing happened. But as they entered the front doorway, Mama leaned into her ear and shouted, "NEW ATTITUUUDE!"

Pal snapped her head to the side and looked Mama directly in the eye. "I hate you. I cannot *wait* until my fourteenth birthday when I can go and live with Daddy. I am counting down the days until I'm out of this -"

S-M-A-C-K!

Mama slapped her across the face. "Go to your room! Go to your room you ungrateful little girl! And you stay in there until your face turns blue!"

Pal stomped upstairs as loudly as she could, with a burning red cheek but not a tear in sight. She made a promise to herself at eight years old to never let Mama see her cry and she was damn near perfect at keeping it. A few incredibly-too-short minutes later, she came back downstairs and plopped herself on the sofa, a smirk across her face. I looked over at her, my eyes grew wide, and I held my breath. Slowly I turned to see our mother's reaction. Mama was the last to see her face, when she finally laid eyes on her she was stunned. My sister had taken all of her blue eye shadow and covered her entire face in it. She came downstairs when her face turned blue. The room was silent.

For as long as I knew them, Mama and Pal seemed more like nemeses than mother and daughter. I didn't understand why Mama couldn't see the funny, brave, and resilient daughter she had. I was told she was jealous of my sister from the day she was born. Daddy said Mama hated how much attention he gave her. Pal was attached to Daddy at the hip. When she was small, long before I was born, she would only let him wash her hair. She would scream if Mama tried to do it.

I also sometimes wondered why Pal was making life so much harder on herself. If she knew Mama was jealous of her, why didn't she try harder to make peace with her? I didn't realize she was surviving with the tools she was given, just like me.

The one thing I learned from their dynamic was that I could not follow in Pal's footsteps. She was gifted with fire and I was gifted with silk. Whatever wrath she endured I would not survive. I knew I could not afford anything our mother might perceive as a threat. Whatever I felt inside, needed to stay inside.

4

GIRLHOOD

One night, when Pal was thirteen and I was seven, we were downstairs watching TV in our usual t-shirt nightgowns. They had Garfield or Snoopy or something on the front, the ones with cheesy quotes printed on them, like *I Hate Mondays*.

We were singing and dancing to whatever was playing on the TV, not an uncommon occurrence for us. Just a moment of free-spirited girldom. Our dance party was interrupted by a moment that changed the way we saw ourselves and shaped how we thought the world saw us forever.

"What are you doing?" Mama asked, in an accusatory tone. This tone was all-too-familiar. It let you know your night was about to go very badly. But which one of us was to blame? My sister and I looked at each other, and then at her, with genuine confusion. It was clear from her eye contact that Mama was speaking to Pal.

"What?" Pal said.

"Why are you parading around the house like that?! Are you trying to get his attention?!" By "his" attention she was referring to Larry, our 40-something year old stepfather whom we found repulsive. We made fun of just about everything about ole Larry. The way he burped every single time he yawned. The fact that he put ice in his milk. The way he always had food stuck in his mustache. Why would my sister want *his* attention? "You're lusting after him! Get upstairs and put some clothes on! You should be ashamed!"

That was the exact word she used. *Lusting*. I had never heard that word before in my life but I somehow knew exactly what it meant the moment it left her lips.

Pal ran upstairs, humiliated, and desperate to make it into her bedroom before the first tear fell. I ran after her. When I got to the bedroom I could see she was trying to hide the fact that she was crying. It was the first time I saw her break her promise to herself.

"Why would she think I'm flirting with *him*?!" she said as she threw our stuffed animals across the room.

I think about this moment often. There are so many layers to the pain. First, to have her developing body commented on at such a young and vulnerable age. Her budding breasts were something she didn't ask for and was already insecure about, and then to have someone accuse her of actually *trying* to make people notice them? And Larry, of all people. I mean, the man drank so much Dr. Pepper he repeatedly gave himself kidney stones but never learned his lesson and picked up a glass of damn water.

Second, to tell a thirteen year old that she was "lusting" after a 40 year-old man. To place that burden on a child for any such inappropriateness that wasn't even happening. Third, for the origin of all that shame, blame, and toxic messaging to be your mother. The person whose job it was to nurture, protect, and love you unconditionally. *That* was the woman accusing her, a young girl who innocently wore a nightgown she'd worn a thousand times before. A girl joyfully dancing with her little sister, unable to conceive of such dark ideas until her mother accused her of them. Mama never apologized for what she said. We were left to sort it all out on our own.

"I hate her. I can't wait to leave here forever." Pal continued to take her frustration out on the stuffed animals, but less so now. She wiped the forbidden tears away.

"I know. I can't wait for you to either, it's just a few more months. I'm sorry. I don't know why she said that." I tried my best to console her.

"I'm sorry I'm going to leave you here alone with her."

"It's ok. I understand."

I wasn't lying. I did understand. I always felt like she had it worse than I did. Sure, she didn't get molested, but I didn't get the brunt of the abuse from our mom. Hers definitely seemed worse to me.

"I can't believe she thinks you'd have the hots for Metroid Man." I said with a chuckle.

"I know!", Pal responded, "The man who constantly spits when he talks and always has strings of spit every time he opens his mouth. Disgusting!"

"It looks just like Bubble Mountain from Metroid inside his mouth. So gross."

We died laughing, that joke never failed to crack us up. We were still the same carefree, dancing girls. Only now we knew to dance quietly and only around each other.

Ever the excellent promise-keeper, Pal moved out exactly on her 14th birthday, the earliest she legally could in the State of Georgia. I learned so much from her while she lived with us. She showed me all of the land mines so that I may step slightly to the side and dodge the explosion. Because she was fire and I was silk. Thanks to her mistake of dancing in a nightgown, once my body started changing I knew to keep it covered. I knew not to dance unless I was alone. I knew how much eye contact was respectful and how much was flirting. Because of her pain, I figured out femininity was dangerous. I dressed in boy's clothes and became the least threatening pubescent girl I could be. And it worked, because I never once was accused of flirting with him. Thank you, Pal, for showing me how to stay safe.

5

CUSSING OUT GOD

"Dear God, - FUCK!". I cleared my throat and let out a hard sigh.

"Dear God, I hope - FUCK!". Another frustrated sigh. *Ok, I've got this.*

"Dear - FUCK!". I took a deep breath and held it for ten seconds. Well, held it for more like 20 seconds because I had to start over a couple of times because I didn't "count it right". Followed by a long exhale from pursed, stressed out lips. I was summoning whatever zen I could muster.

"DearGodIhopeyouredoingwell - FUCK! Gahhhh!!!". I slammed my pillow over my face and let out a silent scream.

Once I learned the F-word, from Eddie Murphy's *Raw* of all places, I couldn't make it through a single prayer as a kid without dropping at least ten to fifteen of them. I was told it was the worst cuss word in the world, which was exactly why I couldn't get it out of my head. The more I thought about *not* saying it, the more my brain said it. I thought I was either possessed by demons or just a very bad person. I wasn't sure which was worse. If I didn't pray I would go to hell, but if I cussed out God that surely would be grounds for hell as well. Damned if you do, damned if you don't. Literally.

Later, I formulated a plan. I noticed that my compulsion to cuss subsided once my prayer got about halfway through. So I would pray to my stepmom's dead parents first. They were nice people but I barely knew them. I would get all of my vulgarity out on them, then I would ask to speak to God once the compulsion to cuss calmed down. Poor Mary and Skip, I'm sorry I cussed ya'll out so much. It was either you or God.

6

PLAY THERAPY

"Cindy, you're going to meet with a nice lady named Mrs. Colleen. She has toys and stuff to play with so it will be fun. She's going to talk to you about your sister moving out and she'll make sure you aren't feeling too sad about it or anything. Ok?" Mama was using her sweet voice but I could tell there was something else just beneath the surface of that sweetness. I obediently nodded my head.

My first attempt at therapy was when I was eight years old. It's not uncommon for eight year olds to see therapists these days, but in the early 90s it was noticeable. I was told I was going to cope with Pal moving to Daddy's house. Which was interesting, because I repeatedly said I was fine with it and happy for her.

"But... remember... you can't talk to her about *the Jesse thing*, ok?"

The Jesse thing. I was shocked she said his name at all but especially in reference to *that*. I nodded my head again, being sure she didn't see the shock on my face at the mention of his name.

"Ok. Because if you *did* tell her they would send police to take you away from me and you'd never see me again -"

"*Mama*, I know. I'm *not*."

"Ok, good. I hope you have a good time."

I nodded one more time and we walked inside the play therapy office.

Even though she was an intense mother, the idea of never seeing her again still made me sad. Plus, I knew that it would destroy her to lose both daughters back-to-back, and I didn't want to cause her that much pain. Extra plus, I did *not* want to talk about *the Jesse thing* ever again with anyone!

The play therapist walked in and she was as sweet as I imagined someone who plays for a living would be. She had a plastic bin filled with rice that felt soothing to run my fingers through. Also in the bin were lots of tiny plastic farm animals. There were even little plastic fences and hay bales to complete the tiny farm theme.

"So tell me about your sister." said Mrs. Colleen.

"She's great. I love her so much. She is my best friend. Also, she has beaten the game Metroid which is very, very hard to do."

"Oh she sounds wonderful."

There was a long pause while I played with the adorable tiny farm animals. I was really falling for the little baby pig.

"You must miss her now that she moved in with your father?" I wasn't shocked she asked me that. Luckily, I had already answered this question about a thousand times before from Daddy, Pal, and Mama so I already had my answer all prepared. Everyone was worried about how much I would miss my sister but me.

"Yes... but it's ok.", I said just as I had rehearsed, "I understand. She will be happier there and that makes me happy for her and cancels out any of my sad feelings."

"Well that is very sweet of you. She is lucky to have someone as mature and kind as you for a sister."

I got back to my pretend farming until it was interrupted yet again by more therapy.

"It's ok if you do feel both happy and sad. It would be understandable, you know."

"I just feel happy." I quipped.

"Ok. Hey, I can see you like the farm animals. Why don't we play pretend with them together?"

Finally, I thought, *the therapy is over and we can have some fun.*

I picked up the little baby pig, "I'll be this one." I had to stake claims on my favorite. "Who do you want to be?"

"I'll be the cow, I like him."

She walked her cow over to my little baby pig.

"Hello there!" said the cow.

"Hello! What are you doing?" said the little baby pig.

"I'm not having a very good day."

"Oh no, I'm sorry Cow. What's wrong?"

"I'm sad, Little Baby Pig. My best friend Donkey just moved away and I miss him."

Wow, this woman will not give up.

I knew we weren't just playing pigs and cows. I felt smart that I cracked the code of play therapy. *This therapist wants me to act my feelings out with these farm animals. Not only that, she seems to want me to feel sad. But, Mama wants me not to be sad.* Mrs. Colleen and Mama wanted two different things from me. I needed to figure out a way to make both of them happy. *I've got it.*

"Oh, Cow, that's terrible," I said, "I'm sad too."

"Oh no! Why are *you* sad, little pig?"

"I'm sad because everyone is mean to me at school..."

I went on to put on the performance of a lifetime. Horses, sheep, and dogs performed an act of bullying so epic Scorcese would be jealous. Little baby pig was treated cruelly and totally left out. I knew Mrs. Colleen would assume the other animals represented people at my school and the little baby pig represented me. I led her down a path of deception because it was easier to be fake sad about a fake thing than real sad about a real thing.

After our play time, Mrs. Colleen, Mama, and I all met together. The two of them discussed my sister leaving and how she thought I was coping quite well. Mama bursted into tears. She may not have wanted me to be sad but somehow me being happy allowed her to be sad. Mrs. Colleen did her best to console her. I thought, *I think she needs this more than I do.* I sat on the couch, dangling my feet next to my sobbing mother. Mrs. Colleen informed her of the possible bullying at school, and to keep an eye on it. We went on our way.

I never went back to play therapy again. I marked it down as a success. I was proud of the fact that I outsmarted an adult and got graduated from therapy in one visit. I was pretty wise for an eight year old, even if that wisdom came at my own expense.

7

INSIDE WORLD

About a year after Pal moved to Daddy's house, Mama and Larry bought a large piece of land and built a log cabin on it. The cabin had two bedrooms, which I thought made it very clear to Pal there was no turning back from her decision to move out. She didn't want to turn back anyway, but I still imagine it hurt.

Pal and Jessie were both gone and now it was just me. I filled the newly abundant amount of alone time with my Inside World. Inside World was a magical place that primarily existed inside my head. When I was alone in my bedroom, I became an actress. I conducted interviews at the fake Cannes film festival for my latest starring role in an indie film that I took for the love of acting and not the money. My films always got rave reviews from critics, and my interviewers were always fascinated with me.

Two things brought my Inside World to life the most. One was music. When I listened to music, I lived a different life to each song. *I Alone* by Live conjured images of dying in the arms of the man I loved. *Scarborough Fair* by Simon & Garfunkel sent me to my cool shared apartment with Pal where we baked pies in aprons together and picked up fresh flowers every day on our way home from our awesome jobs.

Undone by Weezer filled my empty bedroom with friends who all wore sweaters and hung out around campfires and played guitars and told inside jokes, all of which I understood, which was not as familiar of a feeling in real life.

The other place my Inside World came to life most was in nature. It was the only time my Inside World was allowed outside. With acres of woods and fields to frolic in without anyone seeing me, the magic exploded outside of me like a projector on a screen. I could get completely lost with myself and no one could see me. I would build tiny cities out of little sticks and rocks, and then flood them with water to see who survived and who perished. I loved pretending to be an indigenous person tracking and scavenging for my next meal. Streams and rivers were my favorite. I loved running my hands through a flowing stream. The sound of the water drowned out the noises in my head better than anything else, even music. I would be alone in nature for hours every single day. My Inside World was so beautiful, most of the time more beautiful than my real world.

I never shared my Inside World with anyone. I sometimes listened to see if others showed clues of having an Inside World too. But if they did, they were holding that secret close to their chest. And I could understand why. Once it was shared they might try to take it away. I couldn't afford to lose my Inside World because sometimes it was all I had.

If I could be a fly on the wall at any point in my childhood, I would like to spy on myself while alone in nature. Just a little weirdo kid twirling around in the trees with dirty feet and tangled hair.

8

TRAILER TRASH

"Bill, hold still! I don't want to poke your eye out!" Little Mama yelled.

"Good God, woman, you're going to kill me!"

Three of Daddy's sisters were attempting to squeeze him into a blue sequined dress, while his niece was applying press-on nails and his wife was attacking him with mascara and a lash curler. He had a death grip on his Natty Light and took a sip every chance he got.

He was preparing for the Mr. Moonlight pageant. Mr. Moonlight was an annual event where men dressed in full drag and participated in a pageant for charity. His talent was lip syncing *Stand by Your Man* by Tammy Wynette.

"Hold still, Uncle Bill." my cousin said as she violently sprayed glitter into his beard.

There were at least a dozen people crammed into our double-wide trailer attempting to turn Daddy into a beautiful woman. That trailer was always full. Inside lived four adults, 2 teenagers, a baby, and (every other weekend) me. The adults were Bill (my Daddy) and his wife Carol (whom we called "Little Mama" because we loved her too much to call her Carol, plus she was only 5' tall), and my Uncle Mark and his wife Lori (Uncle Mark was Daddy's brother and it just so happened

Lori was Little Mama's best friend - the brothers met the best friends at a nightclub one night after they all had said they swore off serious relationships). Uncle Mark and Aunt Lori had a brand new baby boy, Little Mark. Daddy and Uncle Mark were living together while they helped build each other's houses on a piece of land they bought. The two teenagers were Pal and my half-brother Little Bill. He was 11 years older than me from a previous marriage. His mom sent him to live with Daddy after he got in trouble in school, she said he was "too much for her to handle".

That trailer was always full of people but it never felt crowded. We hosted cousin sleepovers most weekends. We would lay on what we called "pallets" (which was basically a pile of blankets and pillows laid out on the living room floor). You would have to play hopscotch around the bodies if you had to pee in the middle of the night. Daddy's brothers and sisters came over all the time to play canasta or Big Deal (a version of Monopoly for people who couldn't afford Monopoly).

For fun, we would search the property around the trailer for "ancient" artifacts. Our home was on the same land Daddy grew up on, but his childhood home burned down, twice actually, when he was little. He said anything we found would have belonged to him as a child so it was special to him. All we ever found was silverware but it felt like the crown jewels when we discovered it.

The happiest place I ever lived as a child was in Daddy's double-wide trailer. Whenever I pass a trailer that has a tended flower garden or a ridiculous amount of Christmas decorations my heart smiles. I'm convinced that is where all of the happy people are. I can't remember using my Inside World in that trailer. I think the real world there was magical enough.

Daddy placed first runner up in Mr. Moonlight. I think it was the glitter beard that won the judges over.

9

PERKS OF BEING SICK

Some of the best memories I have with Mama were from when I was sick. I would get to stay home from school (because my sick days were always on school days) and watch *The Price is Right*. But better than that, I got pampered by Mama. When I was sick, everything else was better.

Mama worried a lot about everything. She worried about people scheming against her, about bad things happening to me, if her husband was cheating on her, she worried all the time. She always needed something to be wrong. So when I was sick, we all knew what was wrong. She didn't have to speculate, investigate, or accuse. We knew who the culprit was: a stomach bug.

I suspect most of my "stomach bugs" were really anxiety or just made up altogether. But it was worth it, those sick days were glorious. She'd bring me a wet washcloth and put it on my forehead, regardless of if I had a fever. I loved how cool it felt on my skin when she came to rotate it every hour. She made me pancakes and layed with me while I ate them in bed. I felt like royalty.

I wasn't the only one who noticed the perks of being sick around Mama. Larry would get sick all the time too. And I knew he did it for the same reasons I did, because I faked 99% of my stomach bugs and he caught all of them. What were you catching over there, Larry?

When I was ten I had a routine physical at the pediatrician's office. She had me bend over and touch my toes while she slid her fingers up my spine.

"Huh," the doctor said, "Her spine is slightly rotated. It's not scoliosis, but let's keep an eye on it. Be sure she uses good posture at home and stays physically active."

I had the physically active part down, hell I couldn't sit still. But my posture was total crap. But for Mama, all of that didn't matter. She heard that I was doomed.

For the next several months, Mama talked about "my scoliosis". She researched it and constantly speculated on whether it was getting worse. It went on for so long I actually started to believe I had scoliosis. And I loved every second of it. A chronic illness was like a sick day that never ended. I bet Larry was so jealous. Can't catch a crooked spine.

Eventually the topic of my spine fizzled out, I guess it never got any worse and that got a bit boring. But my desire to be chronically cared for never left. I'm not sure what other little kids pretended up in their rooms, but I pretended I was lying in a hospital, dying. The cause of death would change (cancer, car accident, beat up by a gang of hoodlums), but the theme was always the same.

I would stretch the wire from my walkman headphones across my face and hook the jack into my nose. I pretended I was on a ventilator, barely hanging on. I imagined everyone coming to tell me how much they loved me, and Mama coming in to feed me soup and brush my hair every day. Sometimes I would even make it to the funeral before I fell asleep. I'd lie on my bed, arms crossed over my chest in my pretend coffin. One by one, my loved ones would come to pay their respects and say their goodbyes. It was a phenomenal way to fall asleep, to pretend I was in a coma. I was so jealous of those kids in the hospitals. I thought, *They must get so much attention from their moms.*

10

DIRT CHILD

I hated school. It was eight hours a day of being told to be still, patient, quiet, and to pay attention to long boring speeches on a never-ending loop about stuff I wasn't the slightest bit interested in. There was never a time that I loved school. But I never hated it quite as much as when I was in private school.

After Pal moved out, I was sent to LaGrange Academy. I didn't know if it was some attempt at rewarding me for staying when Pal left, but it felt more like a punishment. It was all rich kids, and I hated rich kids. I listened to *Fortunate Son* by Creedence Clearwater Revival a *lot* and took the lyrics as sound life advice.

It was also a lot harder than public school. Everyone bragged about how rigorous the math was and I was confused as to why that was something worth bragging about. I would have been much more impressed by a school that had *easier* math. Plus, if there was anything I didn't need, it was a more rigorous curriculum.

I mostly survived Language Arts because I made up every single book I "read" the entire time I attended school there. Which mostly went unnoticed, so I must've been a pretty good writer afterall. I hope the Pizza Hut *Book It* creators don't read this, they're likely to sue me for all the free pizzas I scammed them out of.

Science was ok because at least we did stuff with our hands from time to time. All of my other classes were total disasters, especially math. I was the dumbest kid in class. I don't say that subjectively. The teachers let their prize students record grades into their grade book, and they inevitably told everyone what they were, and mine were always the lowest. Sometimes I had competition from the kid who was out half of the year because he was in a car accident and had to learn to write with his left hand. Or occasionally from the boy who lived with his grandma and didn't ever speak. But usually mine were the worst.

I'd love to say the reason my grades sucked so bad was because I was distracted by my rich social life, but I wasn't doing much better in that department either. I only got invited to the parties where it was clear the parents made them invite *all* the girls. I always said I was bullied in school, but that wasn't really true. The truth was I *felt* bullied. I was an obvious outsider. I was excited to buy the Garth Brooks replica button down shirt when the other girls were geeking out over jelly sandals. I had a gravel driveway that was a mile long when the other kids knew what the word *cul-de-sac* meant (I didn't know the meaning of that word until I was in my 20s). And I was one of the poorer kids at the rich school. No one was rubbing it in my face or leaving me out to be mean, it was just obvious that I didn't belong. I felt so insecure about how different I was that *I* talked about it constantly in an attempt to prove how much it didn't bother me. And since they thought I was proud of all my weirdness, they went along with it and gave me the nickname *dirt child* (because of how dirty my feet were from walking around barefoot outside all the time). They thought it was hilarious, they thought *I* thought it was hilarious, but in reality it stung.

As much as it sucked, it wasn't as bad as I made it out to be. But, like I learned in play therapy, it served me to have the narrative of being the girl who was bullied. Whenever Mama "sensed" something was wrong, I could always say someone was mean to me at school. Whenever I had an anxiety induced stomach-ache over her and Larry fighting, I could always say it was because someone was mean to me at school. Whenever Mama had a feeling something bad was about to happen, I could conjure up a story about someone being mean to me at school. It became a safe outlet for all of my pain. I apologize to all the innocent classmates whom I threw under the bus, making Mama hate most of you.

11

PANCAKES

I always loved pancakes.

Mama's pancakes were amazing. They were one of the few things she made from a box, Bisquick pancake mix. They were thick and fluffy. She put big fat pads of butter on top of each one right off of the skillet, so much butter the pancake would be soaked through when it was done melting. She cooked them to a light golden brown on a griddle she got for Christmas one year (so she could cook fried rice like they do in the Japanese restaurants). She delivered a big stacked up plate to each person. A giant stack of thick pancakes, dripping with butter. It looked just like the pancake stacks you see in cartoons. She served them with Aunt Jemima syrup, with which I would smother them. I would eat them so fast I could still feel one sliding down my throat as I was shoving the next one in. There would be a pool of syrup and butter left on my plate after I finished my stack, so I would always ask for 1-2 more so as not to waste that concoction of sugary deliciousness.

Little Mama's pancakes were amazing too. She barely cooked anything from scratch but pancakes were on that short list. She made them extra thin, her batter was almost like water. You had to fold them over to make them thick enough to stick with your fork. She made them into shapes, usually of things that were relevant to our life at the time. A four-leaf clover for St. Patrick's Day, for example. Only the first pancake was in the shape of a circle, "the dud" as she would call it, which she would often let me eat it right off the griddle with no syrup or butter or anything. They were always a little burnt because of how thin they were and how long it took to make the shapes. We had to guess the shapes before we could eat them, and we often guessed wrong because it was usually impossible to tell. But how bad they were was part of the fun. She served them with *I Can't Believe It's Not Butter*, the Fabio-endorsed alternative to real butter which tasted like nothing but apparently it was going to save all of us from heart attacks so we just dealt with it. To offset the benefits of the fake butter, we used sugar cane syrup that we bought in bulk every year at the Syrup Soppin' fair in Notasulga, Alabama. You only needed about a dime-sized amount for all of your pancakes because it was so sweet. We all ate cane syrup because of Daddy. He was obsessed with that stuff and put it on just about everything. If you didn't put it on your pancakes he would take it personally and say he failed as a father. All the pancakes were served on one big platter and everyone ate them family-style.

At Mama's house I told her she made the best pancakes ever. At Daddy's house I told Little Mama she made the best pancakes ever. I wasn't lying to either of them, technically. I was two different people at each house. When I said they were the best I ever had, I meant it. It just depended on which version of me was eating them. I wasn't lying to anyone, but it felt like I was lying to everyone. I would lie awake at night as a child wondering which pancakes were the real me.

12

AWARDS

I've won two awards in my life and both of them were in the 5th grade.

The first was when my classmate, McClaine, and I won first place in a lip syncing contest at the school dance. She and I were an odd pair for a lip sync duet. She was an actress. She was a sweet girl, but conversations with her were either about acting or about *her* acting. She missed school all the time to be in Les Miserables or the JC Penny catalog. She brought magazines to school to show us that she was in them. There she was, popping her jean jacket collar, her head tilted to the side, adorned with a floppy hat with a big fat daisy on the front of it. She was polished and poised, she had braces way earlier than the rest of us so her teeth were already pearly white and perfect-looking while everyone else had train wrecks for smiles. She always got the solo at the school concert, which really annoyed me if I'm being honest.

We weren't really friends. We barely spoke. Our circles didn't run together. Her circle was filled with the straight-A students who wore in-style clothing and had their shit together. My circle was (at the height of my popularity) Beth (the girl who played Dead Animals, used an inhaler, and once told me she thought deodorant lasted *at least* 2 days as long as you didn't shower) and Shannon (who was obsessed with 90s grunge and wanted to *be* Kurt Cobain more than she wanted to date him).

But, regardless of the mysterious circumstances of how this came to be, there McClain and I were, the unlikely pair rehearsing dance moves to *Respect* by Aretha Franklin. The competition was a nail-biter. We ended up having to do a 2nd lip sync battle for first place and chose *Joy to the World* by Three Dog Night. We clutched the win when our competitors (a group of boys) did some sexually suggestive hip-thrusting to the B-52's *Love Shack*. The teachers had to intervene, thus, disqualifying our competition. McClaine and I were handed the trophy for the 1993 LaGrange Academy 5th Grade Dance Lip Syncing Competition.

The school didn't plan for the students to perform in groups, so they only made one winner's trophy. When they handed us the cheap, gold painted winged-goddess, McClaine and I looked at each other. I didn't know what she was thinking, but I had never seen anything more beautiful in my life. The idea of not coming home with that trophy made me want to rip the stage apart. I felt the fear/rage build up in my chest. *I picked the songs, I made the dance moves, McClain probably wins so many damn trophies in her life... she gets JCPenney, I want that trophy, Goddammit!*

"You keep it. It's no big deal." McClaine said.

Man, she was a lot better at good sportsmanship than I was. She must have had a lot more experience with it working in the theater. I was ready to rip her head off for that crappy hunk of gold spray painted glory. But the truth was, she was right, it was no big deal to her. People like McClaine won awards all the time. She had whatever that thing was that people have that just made them capable of winning things. Maybe it was charisma, maybe it was *je ne sais quoi*, maybe it was talent. Whatever it was, I didn't have it. The world never fell apart around people like McClaine, it always seemed to just fall together.

The other award I won was 2nd place in the nationwide Brachs Candy *Why I Love My Mother* competition. It was a contest that ran in the early 90s, where people could send in an essay about how much they loved their mother and Brachs would select winners. 1st, 2nd, and 3rd place would receive a box of prizes and a congratulatory letter and their essays would be published in a women's magazine.

I still remember how official the package looked when my prize arrived. On top was a letter of congratulations typed on crisp white card stock with the official Brachs letterhead. The box was filled with free Brachs candy. Admittedly, Brachs is arguably the crappiest of all the major candy companies. Their greatest hits are the really waxy jelly beans and candy corn. Prior to winning, it was the candy I would have avoided at Halloween. But after winning, I became a Brachs spokesperson overnight. Most prized of all, beneath the fancy letterhead and free candy, was a 24k gold (plated) necklace with a 3D pendant of Bugs Bunny. I wasn't sure why Bugs Bunny, I guess Looney Tunes and Brachs collabed in the early 90s.

I was obsessed. I'd never been more proud of anything in my life. I wore that necklace everywhere hoping someone - anyone - would ask me where I got it. It turned out most people weren't that curious about Bugs Bunny necklaces, so that was disappointing.

There was only one place I never wore it: Daddy's house. Because then I would have to explain how I got it. How I won the *Why I Love My Mother* contest. He may have some questions, given every other weekend I cried, vented, or did a comedy bit about how much I hated living with my mother. Also, Pal might have some questions about what I loved so much about our mother. The same mother that I watched make her life a living hell.

Their confusion would have been valid. It was one thing to keep the peace with Mama, it was a very different thing to enter a nationwide contest about loving her so much that I thought she was better than all the other moms in the world. But it wasn't enough just to keep the peace. I needed to stack the odds of not being the target of her next round of paranoia… and it seemed I could never stack high enough.

After Pal left, I didn't have anyone else to worry about taking care of but myself. If she still lived with us, I wouldn't have been caught dead entering that contest. That would be saving one person's feelings by hurting another's. But now that I was on my own, it was time to survive the best I knew how. And I was gifted with silk..

13

SEX ED

"Ok, everyone. Welcome to Sex Education class. My name is Dr. Smith and I am a Gynecologist. That is a doctor that delivers babies and helps women stay healthy. Your school has asked me here so I can talk to you about your changing bodies and answer any of your questions."

The room full of pimple-faced middle schoolers stared anywhere but at each other while their parents sat next to them, elbowing them to pay attention. I was in the 6th grade and Mama brought me to a weekend course about sex and puberty at the private school I attended.

"Here are a few of the changes you may be noticing about your body in the very near future, or maybe even right now..." He pointed to a pair of cartoon adolescents that looked a lot like the guy from the Operation game. Except instead of appendices and hearts they had pubic hair and budding breasts. "Some of you may notice the hair on your underarms, pubic area, and maybe breasts or chest is getting thicker and darker. That is perfectly normal."

"Why do we have pubic hair?" said the one kid in the room who wasn't ashamed to be there, Dr. Smith's daughter Graham. Graham often missed social cues and shared unpleasant information no one asked for. Bless her heart, in retrospect she probably had a healthy sense of self and open conversations with her parents but that shit was weird when we were growing up.

"Good question. We can't say for sure, but pubic hair can play a role in stimulating the genitals of the sexual partner and may aid in preparing for intercourse."

Mama looked like she was hit by a bolt of lightning. She murmured "nah-uh" under her breath and started looking for her purse.

"Grab your things. Let's go." she said. I looked up at her face and knew better than to question her authority. I gathered my pencil and paper, that would have remained blank anyway because I wasn't writing any of that shit down. Then I followed behind her as we scooted past the people in our row, I'm sure only making everything that much more awkward for everyone. "This is not appropriate for children." she told the doctor before walking out the door.

When we got into the car, she began her sermon. "Pubic hair... for *stimulating genitals?!* He's telling this to *children!*" I nodded along because I knew better than to do anything but agree. "That man is sick. *Sick!*" A few more seconds passed, her fingers nervously fidgeted with the steering wheel. "He's trying to encourage kids to have sex! It's disgusting!"

The next day Mama called a Talk Time that was really just her own version of Sex Ed class. We discussed the fact that periods were a curse given to women by God to remind us of how Eve tempted Adam with the forbidden fruit. That pubic hair was for *covering* privates, not stimulating them, because we were supposed to cover our bodies (that's why we started wearing clothes after Adam and Eve, because we just couldn't behave ourselves with all that nudity flying around). And that was about it. There was not a lot of sex discussed in Sex Ed.

A few months later, I started my period in the middle of a field while squatting to pee on the ground. She gave me a pad and explained that tampons were for trashy girls who liked putting things in their vaginas.

And that was that.

14

MONTANA

I had just returned home from a trip with Mama and Larry to Montana. Mama and Larry were obsessed with Montana. They loved how secluded it was. They always talked about how cows outnumbered people in Montana. If a movie ever came out that was filmed in Montana, we would watch it over and over. They wanted to buy land and move out there permanently. Mama once asked Daddy if Larry could adopt me, that way we could just all go be one big happy Montana family together and she would never have to hear his name again. That went about as well as you might imagine it went. Needless to say, Daddy said no.

I was visiting Daddy for the first time since returning from our latest trip to Montana and about to give him the debrief. Debriefs were a play by play of everything that happened at Mama's house since I last saw him. Traditionally, my debriefs about life with Mama were comedy gold. I learned how to spin a tragedy into a comedy at an impressively young age and I was proud of it.

"Tell me everything." Daddy said as he pulled up a chair. He was always ready for the juicy details. He had already gathered from the one phone call I made during the trip that there was tea to be spilled.

"Well… it all started when we went to baggage claim to get our luggage… which never came. We waited for 3 hours and no sign of our suitcases anywhere. The airline lost our bags."

Daddy covered his mouth with his hand. "No. We are clearly not off to a good start."

"Clearly."

"So what did ya'll do?"

"They gave us these little hygiene kits with toothpaste and stuff in them and some money and sent us on our way. They said if our bags show up they'll send them to our cabin. So we left empty handed. When we got to the cabin, there was a hot tub. Mama and Larry were *ooh-ing* and *ahh-ing* all over it. I already knew where this was going. Since no one had any clothes or bathing suits or anything they decided to get in the hot tub *totally naked* while they washed their clothes." I placed a finger over my lips and puffed out my cheeks as if I was barely able to keep myself from vomiting all over the floor.

"Naked?? With you right there? Oh god!"

"Yep. Well, in the next room anyway but there was no door dividing us. I had to sleep on the sofa in the living room because they only rented a one bedroom cabin, so I just planted myself on the sofa and didn't move. Then… they had the bright idea to use the Pert Plus that was in the hygiene kit to make a bubble bath in the hot tub. They were making all these lovey dovey noises, it was disgusting! I don't want to hear that!"

"Oh dear." Daddy said with his face in his palm.

"But that's not all…"

"There's more?!"

"Oh there's so much more. Like a minute after they put the Pert Plus in the hot tub you start hearing screaming. Blood curdling screaming."

"Screaming?" Daddy's face turned from shocked to confused, mixed with a little shameless intrigue. I had his full undivided attention and

I loved it.

"Apparently, something about the shampoo and the chlorine in the hot tub was not a good combination for... uh... someone's... genitals."

His mouth dropped fully open. Several seconds of silence passed as he processed what he'd just heard. Followed by laughter that likely held within it a deep, deep sense of satisfaction. "Oh... my god. I don't even..."

"Yeah... And that's not all. I haven't even talked about the trail ride yet."

"The trail ride?" He was still wiping away tears from the burned genitals story.

"Our trail guide was a woman..."

"Oh no..."

He already knew where this story was going. It was no mystery that Mama was a jealous woman. It always baffled me that she was somehow once married to Daddy. He was not shy to point out any attractive woman he ever saw. But Larry wasn't like Daddy. He followed all of her rules. When a sexy woman came on TV, he covered his eyes and announced "Not looking!". When our server was a woman, he looked at the menu meticulously while Mama ordered for him. Whether Larry was a patient man or a spineless loser, was not really for me to decide. He was who he was.

"The first few miles of the trail ride started off OK. Mama rode behind the guide and Larry was in the back. But at some point his horse insisted on pushing past us and getting right behind the guide. I could tell she was already mad then. Then we came to a cliff. Mama wanted to turn around but the trail guide reassured us that the horses knew what they were doing and we would be safe. Lar (that's what I called him at Daddy's house, always with a sarcastic tone) said 'Let's just stay on the trail' and that was it. She was like, 'Oh so you just want to side with *her* huh?! That's fine, why don't you stay with *her* then.

We're turning around. Let's go, Cindy.' So then she went to turn the horses around and the guide said we couldn't take the horses on our own for liability reasons or something, so if we wanted to turn around we'd have to do so on foot. So we did."

"You're kidding. You *walked* back? How far?"

"I don't know, like five miles… it felt like forever and it was soooo hot."

"I'm sorry, Jack. Are you ok?"

Daddy called me Jack, short for my original nickname, Fatjack. I earned that name when I was little. I used to cover the lower part of my face with my hair to pretend I had a beard like his, and I would puff my stomach out to mimic his slight beer belly. I wanted to look just like him. He told me I was a little Fatjack, just like he was. As I got older he dropped the "Fat" part, probably because it didn't go over very well in public for people to hear a father call his daughter fat. It never bothered me.

"Yeah, I'm ok. It was funny but it was also rough. I did cry one time on the trip, they couldn't see me. In the backseat of the car. They were fighting and I just started missing you. I'm just so sick of living there."

He put his hand on my shoulder. "Just a few more months. It'll be over in just a few more months."

In seven months I would be turning fourteen and, like Pal did six years prior, I would legally be able to decide which parent I wanted to live with. It had been my plan all along to go live with Daddy. I waited six long years but this last year felt the longest. Even though this was always the plan, Mama had no idea. Pal made it loud and clear she was moving out at fourteen from the moment she knew she could, but I wasn't Pal. I still had absolutely no idea how I was going to tell her I'm leaving her after years of telling her how much I loved her.

15

THANKSGIVING

I loved Thanksgiving. It was the one holiday I always had with Daddy, non-negotiable. Even Mama agreed the Garrett's were where I belonged on Thanksgiving. They were a huge family, riddled with tragedy and just as much love. And, boy, could they cook.

To fully understand and appreciate the Garretts, it's important to know a little of their backstory. My grandfather (John Wilson Garrett) and grandmother (Mildred Garrett) met when she was 14 and he was 21 (not uncommon for that generation, but still creeps me out). Apparently, she lied about her age when they met and I'll just have to take my grandfather's word for it he didn't know she was lying. They lived with my grandmother's family and worked as sharecroppers until they could afford to buy a place of their own. They built a grocery store/restaurant called "The Casino" (pronounced ka-SEE-nuh) and lived in the attic above it. At night it turned into a speakeasy. They pushed the tables, chairs, and shelves against the wall to make a dance floor and patrons came to cut a rug. I always heard about how good of a dancer my grandfather was. They had eight children together (one of which they lost at age three to Leukemia, baby Kim). My grandmother died in her 40s from cancer, while half of the children still lived at home, leaving my grandfather to finish raising them as a single dad. It wasn't that he didn't rise to the task, but he was an alcoholic, which left him unable to support them in the way they needed. Wherever he fell short, the kids had to pick up the slack. This created a special bond between all of the Garrett siblings.

The oldest was Ann, the matriarch. Ann's hugs were like being wrapped in a warm blanket. She had hot flashes for what seemed like her entire life, so every time she gave you a kiss your face would be covered with sweat. Garrett Thanksgiving was held at her ex-husband Oz's house. They divorced before I was born, but they remained close and never remarried to anyone else.

Daddy (Bill) was the 2nd oldest sibling and the eldest boy. He answered to Ann, and everyone else answered to him. He was funny and loving but he was tough. He liked things done a particular way. His banana sandwiches had to have 9 slices of banana perfectly aligned, his fried pork chops were only eaten at room temp, and spaghetti was always served with a side of pear salad. (pear salad: a canned pear half filled with mayonnaise in the center and sprinkled cheddar cheese on top - a Southern delicacy but it always made me gag). With no formal education beyond 10th grade, he started his own construction company with his two brothers and exchanged a reliable paycheck for more freedom and time with his family. He did not live to work, he worked to live. An example I am grateful to have witnessed up close and I have carried with me throughout my life. All of the Garrett men were considered handsome, but he was the most handsome of them all and he knew it. He often used his looks to get what he wanted. He had piercing green eyes set in thick, dark eyelashes and he had a strong, handsome nose and dark tanned skin. Everybody talked about those eyes. I got his green eyes. Jackpot.

Uncle Don was 3rd in line and Daddy's best friend. He was a softie. Don did whatever you asked and never said a harsh word to anyone...

ever. When he was a little boy, he accidentally started a fire while playing with matches and burned their home to the ground (one of two times the Garrett's childhood home burned down). He never forgave himself and I think, in his sweetness, he was trying to make up for it the rest of his life.

Next was Aunt Debbie. I thought Debbie was mean when I was younger but later realized what a badass she was. When my grandmother died, Debbie was the oldest sibling still at home. She had to step up and raise the remaining younger children. There wasn't a time in her life she wasn't taking care of someone and yet you never heard her complain.

After her came Uncle Mark. He was the funny one. The kids in the family loved him because he was goofy and told hilarious stories. Daddy always accused him of exaggerating his stories but he would never admit to it. He and Aunt Lori were who we lived in the trailer with while the brothers helped build each other's houses.

The next to last sibling was Aunt Tami. She was full of energy and impossible not to love. She was the butt of everyone's jokes because she was ditzy. But I knew she was never as ditzy as she seemed. I think she just allowed herself to be the butt of the joke because it brought people together in laughter. Everyone said I was just like her.

The baby of the family was Wina (short for Edwina). Wina was a nut in the best way. She struggled with addiction and wrestled with her sexuality but her heart was solid gold. She was so loving and so incredibly tough.

The Garretts were equal parts magic and tragic. By that Thanksgiving of 1995, when most of them were in their 30s and 40s, they had already survived two childhood homes burning down, lost a baby sibling, and a mother and father. Every tragedy only seemed to make them closer. They created a genuine kind of love together that most people go a lifetime without experiencing. I think the tragedy must be

51

part of the magic somehow.

Thanksgiving of '95 was special because Little Bill came. My half brother, Little Bill, had been estranged from Daddy since shortly after we moved out of the trailer and into the house. He had gotten his girlfriend pregnant and shortly after fell into a drug addiction.

One of the only times I ever saw Daddy cry was after he got home one night from trying to help Little Bill for the last time. The local Sheriff called Daddy and told him they found Little Bill living with a group of drug addicts in an old abandoned shack down by the river. The Sheriff said he would let Little Bill off the hook as long as he went home with Daddy. Daddy told him the only way he would bring him home is if they went straight to rehab right then and there. Little Bill chose jail. They didn't speak again for a couple of years.

Eventually, Little Bill did get clean. I guess he finally reached a point where he felt like he could face Daddy again, so he came to Thanksgiving. When they saw one another, they started with some awkward conversation, which led to a handshake, which led to a hug.

"I'm proud of you son." Daddy said.

"Thank you, Daddy."

"Why don't you come around next weekend too? We're gonna paint Uncle Don's house." Most of our weekends were spent helping one of the siblings get odd jobs done, so this was Daddy's way of offering for Little Bill to hang out.

"Yeah, that sounds alright." Little Bill said with a proud smile, his eyes a bit glossy.

For the rest of Thanksgiving it was as if no time had passed. We all ate turkey and dressing until we were about to puke, and then topped it off with banana pudding and pecan pie. We made fun of each other in the way that only people who truly love one another can. And then, once it was dark outside, it was time to head home. As we pulled away from Oz's I felt sad. I wouldn't see the Garretts again until the 4th of

July at Debbie's house.

Six days later...

"Cindy?" Mama called for me from downstairs.

"Yeah?" I answered.

"Can you come down here?"

I walked downstairs. I sensed the nervousness in Mama's voice but I couldn't for the life of me think of what I had done to cause it.

"Your dad had to be rushed to the hospital."

"Is he ok?"

"I don't know. I think so. I'm not sure. Get dressed, I need to take you down there." I fell into her arms and started crying. I rushed to get ready but it felt like no matter what I did everything moved in slow motion.

In the car on the way to the hospital, the radio played *Have I Told You Lately (That I Love You)* by Rod Stewart. My heart dropped and I wondered, *Is Daddy dead? Is he sending that song to me?* I shook the thought out of my head and was pissed at myself for even thinking like that. But I did make a mental note to remember the song just in case.

When we arrived at the hospital, my Uncle Mark took me from Mama, put his arm around me, and led me down a hall that felt endless. I wasn't used to seeing him so serious.

"Is Daddy ok?" I asked him. But no reply.

Finally, we made it into a little private room, I didn't know hospitals had those. Inside were all of the magical Garretts. I could still feel their magic, only it felt different. Little Mama walked up to me, put both hands on my shoulders, and looked me right in the eye.

"He's gone, sweetheart. He's gone."

16

GARRETT FAMILY DRESSING RECIPE

Here is the best Southern dressing recipe you will ever find.

Cornbread for Dressing:
1 cup self rising meal
1 cup self rising flour
2 eggs
1 1/4 cup buttermilk
1/4 cup melted butter - (preheat in cast iron skillet)
Bake at 425 degrees until golden brown, about 20-25 min.
Cool and then crumble in a large bowl.

Biscuits for Dressing:
1 cup self rising flour
2 tbsp butter or Crisco
½ cup buttermilk
Bake at 400 degrees for about 10-15 min.
Cool and then crumble with the dressing.

Dressing:

Crumbled Cornbread and Biscuits
Saute 1/2 yellow onion and celery
Chopped green onion
2 cans cream of chicken soup
3 eggs (slightly beaten)
Chicken broth (about a cup, just to get to right consistency)
Mix ingredients together and refrigerate until ready to bake

When ready to bake:
Add more chicken broth if the mixture seems thick.

Place 1 stick of butter in the cake pan while oven preheats to 375

Once the butter melts, pour in the cornbread mixture and smooth out

Bake at 375 degrees for about 45 min. until the center is firm and the edges are brown.

17

THE BURYING

We don't know how Daddy died. His heart just stopped. The autopsy said "Cause of Death: Unknown/Sudden Cardiac Death". Losing him fractured me in a way I didn't know a person could be broken. I spent the large part of my childhood working as hard as I could to see patterns, make predictions, and prepare for outcomes, all in an effort to prevent missteps that would result in pain. I stacked odds and had plans, and backup plans, and backup plans for the backup plans. But in the end, when he died I learned that you can do everything and it still wouldn't be enough.

Fun Facts About Losing a Parent During Puberty:

Seeming fine was my biggest priority. I was feeling the most intense emotions of my life during a time when I wanted to make the world think I didn't have any emotions at all. I projected "chill, that's cool, no biggie" energy, while my pain screamed from underneath my skin. And that was before I had a dead dad. I coped by caretaking. I showed everyone I was "so chill and cool" with my dad dying by asking if *they* were ok or if *they* needed anything. Everyone commented on how mature I was, which let me know my plan was working perfectly.

Shame had new, inescapable access to my life. I was a hardcore Christian at the time of Daddy's passing (which only grew more intense after he died because I desperately needed to believe I would see him again). I was confident Daddy was in heaven. Watching me. All the time. All the freaking time. During my budding adolescence. I asked him to please not watch me when I was in the bathroom and desperately hoped that I could actually make deals with people in heaven.

Everyone tried to be my new father. Uncles, family friends, church members, men eager to date Little Mama, and many more stepped up to try and be my new father figure. Some of the contestants felt so pressured to fill the role they disappeared from my life completely because the task overwhelmed them so much (when in reality I just wanted them to stay the same as they were before he died). Some were absolutely not candidates but thought they should be and imposed a lot of unwanted lectures and "wisdom" on me. And the best candidate of all was a sleeper hit. Without trying and with no hidden agenda, he was amazing, unassuming, and exactly the next-best thing to still having Daddy around. I'll talk about him more later.

In school I would forever be the kid with the dead dad. Nothing was more traumatic and ill-timed in an 8th grade classroom than having every adolescents' worst fear come true for one of the students. I wondered sometimes how many kids I scarred for life when they realized their dad, too, could die. I wondered what the teachers said to everyone before I came back to school. I bet they gave them the same speech we got after this kid Simon's grandmom died. They told us to be extra nice to him and not ask him a lot of questions about it. When I returned to school, the teachers, who previously hated me, tiptoed around me. They basically handed me good grades for not killing myself. I'm not sure my grades were ever as good as they were after Daddy died. Everyone treated me like a victim. Even Andrew, the kid who used to swipe his finger up my back and yell "No bra!", was being nice to me. I used to imagine myself laying in a hospital bed getting pitied by everyone I knew. But now that it was actually happening, it wasn't as fun as I had imagined.

The only perk of all this pity was I got to skip PE to see the school counselor. Skipping PE in the 8th grade is like winning the lottery. Especially for me. I notoriously forgot to bring my gym clothes home to wash so I was constantly having to re-wear sweat-soaked clothes that were stuffed in an airtight duffle bag overnight. Plus I could never keep up on the leg shaving and those gym shorty shorts let everyone know how far behind I was.

The school counselor was so sweet, I hate that I cannot remember her name. This was my 2nd therapist so I already felt like a pro. I knew she'd want me to be sad, but I couldn't be too sad, because I instinctively knew Mama did not want to hear from her about how I was crying over Daddy at school. Mama avoided the subject of his death. I'm sure it was hard. Here was the man she hated most in the entire world, and he was finally dead! But in his dying he became a martyr, her child would forever worship him. I think comforting me about his death was painful for her. I related it to the time this girl that I hated at school broke her arm and overnight everyone was her best friend and wanted to sign her cast, do her favors, and pay lots of attention to her. That sucked.

"How are you holding up?" the school counselor asked.

"I'm ok. I'm sad, I miss my dad, but I'm ok."

"I know. I'm so sorry. I can't imagine how you feel. Just remember, grief is love - it's just the hardest expression of it. Have you been reading the book I gave you?"

"Yep."

No I hadn't. She gave me *Chicken Soup for the Grieving Soul.* Those Chicken Soup books were all the rage in the 90s. They were books filled with uplifting stories and sage life advice, and were great if you wanted life advice shoved down your throat by way of toxic positivity and just-love-Jesus. They had one for every person or occasion. *Chicken Soup for the Teenage Soul* for kids in puberty. *Chicken Soup for the Women's Soul* for sad women. *Chicken Soup for the Mother's Soul* if those sad women were moms. My favorite was *Chicken Soup for the Prisoner's Soul* that promised if you just loved God and thought positive things prison would suck a lot less.

I stopped reading that book within the first chapter. It talked about the stages of grief and how anger was one of them. I couldn't imagine being angry at Daddy and I didn't like the implication that I had to be in order to ever have a chance at feeling happy again. Being angry in order to be happy made zero sense to me.

"Do you still feel like you have a good support system at home?" she asked.

"Yes I do."

I could have just stopped there. But when you have something to hide you always keep going.

"My mom and stepmom are very close, they're practically best friends. We all get together all the time to have dinner. We all miss him so much. We play board games we used to play with him and share funny stories about him and stuff."

None of this was even close to true. Mama hated Daddy and if there was one person on the planet she hated more, it would be Little Mama. From visitation, to the funeral, and through the two weeks I stayed with Little Mama and Pal after his death, she and Mama never spoke to one another. Not once.

I didn't know why I felt the need to go above and beyond to paint such a lovely picture of togetherness for my therapist. Maybe I was just saying what I thought she wanted to hear. Maybe I was saying what I wish was true.

18

CHRISTMAS

One month after Daddy passed away it was Christmas time. The first two weeks after he passed I got to stay with Pal and Little Mama. Those two weeks were actually really nice. We all slept in the same bed together, we cried together, and we didn't have to worry about anything but being sad. But after I returned to Mama's house it felt like it was time to get back to normal.

My dream of moving in with Daddy, a dream I never got around to telling Mama, died along with him. I tried hard to accept my new truth. Pal made it out, but I was never going to.

Larry's family was visiting for Christmas. They were the dullest family on the planet. They reminded me of those people who lived in communes and believed the devil was trying to brainwash you through your TV. His nieces wore matching prairie dresses at a ridiculously old age and they always said "Sir" and "Ma'am" which made me look bad. None of them knew Daddy, much less cared about him being gone, so everyone in the house acted like it was a normal Christmas, because for them it was.

Watching everyone else's world not be shattered made me start to feel dizzy, so I went for a walk outside. My Inside World came out and tried to catch its breath.

I started thinking about how this was my first Christmas without him. *I wonder if he bought me any gifts already that I will be able to open on Christmas. Or have I already received the last gift he'll ever give me? What was the last gift he gave me?* I thought long and hard but couldn't remember. *I'm so selfish for wondering about gifts. I should care more about his last words to me.* Then I tried to remember what his last words to me were. But I didn't know they would be significant, so I couldn't make them come to mind. *Why didn't I pay more attention? Why didn't I appreciate him more when he was here?* The shame and longing overwhelmed me and I started to cry.

I headed towards the house because I really needed a hug. One of those nurturing sick day hugs. This was so much worse than being sick. I walked up to the front door and rang the doorbell because I was too embarrassed to cry in front of Larry's family. I knew Mama would answer if the doorbell rang, she wouldn't risk Larry potentially answering the door to a gorgeous saleswoman. She opened the door and saw me standing there with my eyes puffy and swollen with tear streaks down my cheeks.

"What's wrong?" she said.

"I just miss him so much!" I fell into her arms and buried my face into her chest, sobbing. She held me, frozen, I could hear her stuttering and not sure what to say.

"Y-Y-Y-You're going to ruin Christmas. Stop crying!"

I picked my head up and looked up at her, bewildered at her response.

"I can't!" Now I started crying even harder. I could now understand why Pal promised herself to never cry in front of her. She could be so nurturing or she could be so cold, and you never knew which to expect.

She let out a big, frustrated sigh, grabbed me by the hand, pulled me through the house and into her bedroom, quickly closing the door behind her.

"It has been over a month. It is time to move on now. My mom died unexpectedly, too, and I had to move on, so you can too."

"But it's the first Christmas without him! Can I call Pal?"

"I don't think that's a good idea. In fact, I think her and *Little Mama* (who's name she always said with great discomfort) are making you sadder. I'm not sure it's good for you to see and talk to them anymore."

I felt like a giant thumped me in the chest, knocking the wind out in one subtle blow. They were the only lifeline I had and the only people who were hurting the way that I was. My fear turned to anger, her threat to take them away pushed me past a point I had been before with her.

"You *can't* take them away from me! They are all I have and it's the *only* place I am happy!" I defiantly grabbed the phone. She grabbed it too and wrestled it out of my hands.

"That is it. Clearly talking to them is upsetting you and making you worse. This is not the Cindy I know. You are not going to see them again."

Mama finally had permission to set a boundary she wanted to set since the day he died. She took me upstairs, sat me down on my bed, and yanked the phone out of my room. Which was actually a smart move, because I was definitely going to call them as soon as she left.

19

TRUTH OR DARE

After being forbidden from calling Little Mama, Pal, or anyone on Daddy's side of the family, I had no idea how to move forward. My first plan was to kill myself. I went to Mama's medicine cabinet and looked for options for doing the deed. I wondered how much Tylenol or Midol it would take to end a person's life. We didn't have Google back then, so I had to guess. I finally decided the margin for error was a little too high for my comfort level. I didn't want to end up a vegetable and live forever in an even more miserable state. I didn't have the guts to shoot or hang myself, so I decided suicide probably wasn't the route for me.

My backup plan was to tell the truth. The Monday after Christmas break, I skipped PE once again and went to my daily school counselor's meeting. Without warning, I started telling her everything.

"I've been lying to you this *entire* time. My mom and my stepmom are *not* best friends. They hate each other. My mom won't let me speak to her or my sister anymore because she said they're making me too sad. But if I can't see them I don't know what I'll do. I already looked in the medicine cabinet to see what I could take to not be here anymore. My mom is so emotionally abusive and controlling. She always has been. She told me I should be over my dad's death by now. I'm miserable there. I was supposed to move out when I turned 14 but then Daddy died… I was *so* close…" I had no other choice but to let the tears flow freely.

She sat across from me, stunned.

"I'm not lying. I swear I'm not lying," I told her. I was terrified of her not believing me and not only sending me back home, but telling Mama what I said.

"I believe you. It's going to be ok. I'm going to help you." she said.

In the weeks and months following, she never uttered a word of this to Mama. She allowed me to make calls to Little Mama and Pal during our appointment time. She arranged secret meetings between me, Little Mama, and a lawyer to discuss our options for her getting custody of me. She took huge risks in order to help me. I may have forgotten her name, but I will never forget her.

After several meetings and a lot of brainstorming, the lawyer ultimately concluded that there was no solid case to take Mama to court for custody. He said judges like for kids to stay with their biological parents, especially biological moms, and emotional abuse would be too hard to prove. The only remaining option we had at this point was to go to her and ask her to relinquish custody on her own free will. He said it would be a long shot.

20

THE LONG SHOT

By May we had a plan for the long shot. Like a scene straight out of Ocean's Eleven, me, the Garretts, Little Mama, and Pal formulated a plan to ask Mama to relinquish custody. I asked her if I could have lunch with Pal and she reluctantly agreed. After lunch, Pal planned to come inside when she dropped me off and talk to Mama about how unhappy I was there and explain that I wanted to come live with her and Little Mama. Meanwhile, Little Mama would be camped out at my Uncle Don's house because he only lived five minutes away. They knew things could get ugly so they wanted to be able to get there quickly if it did. I had his phone number in my pocket and they would be waiting by the phone.

Pal hadn't been inside Mama's house in years and they hadn't spoken in just as much time. Pal walked to the door with me and, when Mama opened it, she asked, "Can I talk to you?"

"Sure." Mama said, hesitantly.

"Let's go to your bedroom."

They walked into the bedroom and I sat on the couch in the living room, across from Larry. He was sitting in his recliner being his normal doofus self.

66

"Did ya'll have a good time?" Larry asked, clueless as usual. Or maybe he knew something was up and was baiting me for answers, I could never tell how bright he was.

Jesus Christ, Larry. Not now. I thought. *Read the room.* My heart was beating in my ears, I didn't even bother replying to his question. I just listened out for sounds that would indicate how their conversation was going.

I didn't make this an easy job for Pal. My primary survival strategy over the last six years since she left had been to pretend like nothing was wrong. I thought this was going to be my home for the rest of my life, so I focused on making myself as comfortable as possible. And the only way to do that was by making Mama as comfortable as possible. This news was going to come as somewhat of a shock to her.

Just then, I heard their voices getting louder and louder. That was expected. The bedroom door swung open. Mama was trying to shove Pal out. That was not expected.

"No! No! No! Get her out of here! Absolutely not! Leave! Larry! Get her out of here! She is trying to take Cindy away! They are trying to brainwash her to move out!" she screamed as she rammed and shoved my sister out of her bedroom and towards the door.

I stood up and immediately started crying, I could barely see through my tears as I ran after Pal. There was no way I could let her leave me here alone.

"No Mama," I said, "Please! They aren't brainwashing me. I want to live with them, *please* just let me!"

"Absolutely not! Larry! Get her *out*!"

Larry, who was still trying to put the pieces together, blindly obeyed as he always did. He was over six feet tall and 225 lbs. He put his arms around Pal's waist, lifted her up, and started dragging her towards the front door. She fought with everything she had to resist him. Mama had me around the waist, pulling me away from her. Pal braced her arms on both door jams. Larry took her arm and shoved it into submission.

S-N-A-P!

Pal let out a scream that was different from all the other screaming in the room. "You broke my arm! He broke my arm!" She looked around, panicked.

We would find out later at the hospital that he snapped her humerus (the upper arm bone) completely in half. She was doubled over in pain, everyone was in complete shock. In the most horrible way possible, at that moment Mama became a mother again. She stopped fighting and immediately told everyone to get in the car so we could go to the hospital. I had never seen her be more maternal to my sister as she was then. I think she knew it had all gone too far.

Social services separated all of us at the hospital to get our statements. I looked at the scratch on my hand from Mama as I waited for my turn. I promised myself I would not let that scratch heal. I would make it turn into a scar so I would know it really happened. I kept my promise.

When they talked to me I knew I had to tell the whole truth. I had always left it to Pal to fight my fights for me, and I had immense guilt for where that had gotten her this time. I had to find the courage to talk. I was finally speaking my mind but it felt like too little too late. Why had it taken this long before I could do it? I was placed in a temporary foster living situation while the state tried to figure out what to do with me.

Little Mama called her lawyer. He said, "This is the long shot. This is your miracle." We threatened to press charges against Larry unless she signed over legal custody. She really had no other choice. Within a couple of weeks I was gone, and she had lost both of her daughters.

When I arrived at Daddy's house (which was now Little Mama and

Pal's house... or I guess *my* house) for the first time, they had "It's a Girl!" signs everywhere. They made a big deal of my arrival. I finally made it, two weeks before my 14th birthday and six months after Daddy died. I just knew that now everything was going to be ok.

I sat down next to Pal, her arm in a cast. I didn't know if I could handle telling her how sorry I was for what I caused so I didn't say anything at all.

"It was worth it," she said. "It's what got you out of that house."

I laid my head on her shoulder and tried not to let her see me cry.

II

OTHERSIDE

21

TOOTHLESS

"Well? What do you think?" the dentist asked, as he gave me a handheld mirror.

I looked in the mirror and gave it a wide smile, then turned my face side to side. I couldn't believe what I was seeing. I slid my tongue across my new, smooth pearly whites. For the first time in my life, at the age of fourteen, I had a full set of teeth.

"I love them!" I exclaimed.

I was born with a mild cleft palate that resulted in hypodontia (i.e., congenitally missing teeth). My two incisors, the teeth on either side of my front teeth, simply didn't exist. It wasn't noticeable during elementary and early middle school when everyone's teeth were falling out of their head. But by late middle school it had become incredibly noticeable and a major source of embarrassment. Everything about awkward adolescence was magnified by those damn missing teeth.

During the summer after middle school, the same summer I moved in with Pal and Little Mama, the dentist made me a partial denture. It was a plastic plate that fit in my mouth like a retainer, except it had two very perfect, very fake teeth on it. I couldn't wait to show my new teeth off to the world. It was perfect timing. I was about to start high school and I was not only changing schools, I was changing lives. New school, new home, even a new mom. It was the perfect time to reinvent myself if there ever was one. And now I had the perfect smile to go with my new perfect life.

I was technically supposed to remove the partial to eat and sleep, to prevent it from breaking and my gums from turning into an inferno of inflamed redness due to lack of oxygen. But I never took that thing out, only for a brief moment to clean it when I brushed my teeth. I brushed right over those engorged bloody gums, winced a little from the pain, and then immediately popped that retainer back in.

It never broke when I was in public, but I worried about it every second of every day. It did break a couple of times while I was at home, followed by a massive panic attack and refusal to leave the house until it was repaired. I carried super glue around in my backpack just in case, even though my dentist had made it clear: "If it ever breaks, please, whatever you do, do not - I repeat do *not* - super glue it back together."

My teeth were like everything I was hiding at the time. My grief, my changing body, my trauma, my insecurities… everything. Inside, I was holding it all together with a flimsy piece of plastic. But as long as I looked normal on the outside, my secret of not being normal was kept safe. But as much as I pretended to be a normal human, I was in fear of being found out, for the thin piece of plastic to break and everyone see I was a fake.

22

PANTIES AND SOGGY PILLS

"So, what is going on, Cindy? Why aren't you taking the medication I prescribed you?"

Shortly after I moved in with Little Mama and started high school, I was tested for ADHD. That was one test I passed with flying colors. It was recommended that I go on medication, so I began seeing a psychiatrist by the name of Dr. Desai. It was a reasonable assumption that I had plenty of reasons to see a psychiatrist. But, oddly, we never discussed any of those reasons. We didn't talk about living with Mama or dying with Daddy. All we ever discussed were my grades, my messy room, or what medication adjustment we were making that month.

I was on Prozac and Adderall for most of high school. I knew the Adderall was for ADHD but no one ever told me why I was on Prozac. I hated taking my medication. It made me feel like a zombie. It made me compliant, I remembered all my chores and did all my homework, but the trade-off was feeling like all the color had drained out of the world and that life was pointless. People at school even noticed when I took my meds, and they hated it too. I was boring as hell on those meds.

I also never liked the idea of depending on medication to function.

I felt confident I could find a way to work with who I naturally was. Medication was a shortcut, and I was always more of a meandering path that may or may not lead off a cliff kind of girl.

So, in an act of protest, I did everything I could to avoid taking my meds. At first, I just didn't take them. Easy peasy. But then Little Mama started to notice the pill bottle was still full when it was refill time. So I altered my plan and took them out of the bottle but put them in my pockets. That worked, until she found a bunch of capsules and pills rolling around in the laundry. So she started making me take them in front of her, prison-style, where I had to open my mouth and show her it was empty. So then I learned how to hide them under my tongue like a pro. I spit them out in my underwear drawer because I was scared she would find them in the trash. Turns out, nowhere was safe, because one day she found my drawer full of panties and soggy pills. That's when she really lost it. She took me to see Dr. Desai to see what the hell she was supposed to do with me.

Dr. Desai was not my favorite. I'm not sure if I was expecting therapist-level support from a psychiatrist or if he just sucked ass. He gauged my progress on everything *except* how it felt to be me. Good grades, doing chores, following rules, and pleasant to be around - those were the only goals he had for me and therefore those were the only things he cared about. I don't think he ever once asked what *my* goals were. But, if I'm being totally honest, I probably would have just said I had the same goals he did.

"I don't know." I said, "I just hate how the medicine makes me feel."

"Yes, but, do you see how it helps you? How it helps you get your school work done? And your room clean? Don't you want to be able to do those things?" Every sentence he said ended like he was asking a question and that annoyed the hell out of me because I'm pretty sure he was never really asking me anything.

"Sure, but I feel like I can figure out a way to do those things without the medication."

"Psh!" Little Mama interjected. She always sat in on my sessions with him. "How is that working so far? I have put up lists, and reminded you about the lists, and you *still* don't do anything. Your room is filthy. There are bowl*s* - plural - of curdled milk. I even had to put a note on the toilet and you still don't flush it! It's disgusting!" She threw her hands up and let out a hard sigh. "Dr. Desai, does this seem like normal behavior to you? I'm just not sure this is normal behavior, even for someone with ADHD. I mean, *I* have ADHD and I take my meds and have no issues. I just don't get why she *chooses* to be a disaster!"

Less than a year after moving in with Little Mama, she was starting to lose patience with me. To be fair, this was not what she signed up for. She adopted a very different child than the one she ended up with. Before Daddy died, she really only saw "every other weekend Cindy", and she was lovable as hell. That Cindy was hilarious and entertaining, plus a massive people pleaser. Who cares if I forgot to tie my shoes and had a spaced-out look on my face half of the time, I was cute. I made up for my quirks by being cuddly and telling everyone how much I loved them all the time.

The version of me she got would get constant complaints from teachers and needed endless reassurance. I couldn't sleep due to exhausting thought loops that ran through my head at night and a healthy dose of crippling anxiety. She had to wake me up six times every morning. Every single day, I would roll over onto the floor at the side of my bed where she couldn't see me so it would look like I had gotten up and then proceed to fall back asleep on the floor. I hoarded candy in my room and, when I was obviously caught, still lied about it. In a nutshell, I was *a lot*.

She wasn't equipped for this version of me. She didn't have her own biological children. She worked in education her entire life so she raised me like she taught her students. She had high expectations for academic achievement and prioritized fulfilling my potential, two things I sucked at.

"I do not believe this behavior is normal. Her refusal to take medication and defiance in hiding the medicine indicates there are other issues." replied Dr. Desai.

The subject of me being normal or not normal came up in front of me all the time. It always felt like she and Dr. Desai were already on the same page. I often wondered if they talked about me ahead of time behind my back.

"Are you doing drugs?" he asked.

If I had had any liquid in my mouth I would have done a spit take. "Drugs?!"

"Yes. It is a reasonable explanation for why you continue this level of defiance. My recommendations would otherwise be working."

"No, I'm not doing drugs!"

"It is common for people with ADHD to abuse drugs in order to self-medicate. Are you self-medicating?" he asked again.

I looked at Little Mama, to see if she mirrored my shock, but instead she seemed to have already heard this theory before and made up her mind that it was correct. Then I looked back at Dr. Desai, who was likely the one who had already shared this theory with her.

I didn't answer, I just got up and walked away. I knew I lied about a lot of shit, but nothing hurt worse than when I was telling the truth and no one believed me. I wasn't doing drugs. I had never done a single drug in my life. Growing up in a meth and opioid infested town, I had plenty of opportunities. By my Senior year, I had been offered just about everything under the sun. But I had always said no and I was really proud of that. That just made it sting even harder.

23

ATTEMPTING FRIENDS

"Do you want to come to my house and sleep over?"

Sally (who's name has been changed to protect the normal), a very cool girl at my high school, invited me to a sleepover with her and her best friend, Daisy (another normal whose name I am protecting), an even cooler girl at my high school. Not only was I excited to be given the rare privilege of being their third wheel, I was also excited to be attending my very first cool-girl sleepover. Up until this point, any girl who invited me to a sleepover was either a total dork, or had to because her mom didn't want to hurt anyone's feelings.

"Yeah, sure." I said, making sure to sound extra nonchalant about it.

"Great. We can all go to the baseball game together to look at the guys in tight pants and then hang out at my house."

The stars were aligning. Years of playing it cool, acting chill, and being just the right amount of everything and not too much of anything had finally paid off. I had to nail this sleepover in order to solidify myself as a normal, dare I say cool, girl. Cool was normal on steroids.

The day finally arrived, and Sally greeted me at the door of her gorgeous home. "Come on in. Just take your shoes off, my parents don't like when people wear shoes inside."

Her house was massive. She lived in a neighborhood, which was the epitome of wealth in Manchester, Georgia. Her carpet was the riskiest shade of almost-white beige I had ever seen. To be that confident that either (1) no one would mess up your carpet, or (2) you could easily afford to replace it if they did, really screamed big money to me.

She had one whole room just for her cockatoo, who lived in a giant, ornate cage in the center of the room. Sally took him out of the cage and let him rest on her shoulder. I had never seen such a boss move.

"This is Peaches. We've had him my whole life. Don't try to touch him. He's mean to anyone he doesn't know."

"He loves me." Daisy chimed in.

"Yeah, he loves Daisy." she said.

Daisy petted Peaches, establishing dominance over me. I heard her loud and clear. I wanted to tell her there was no competition here, I was just glad I was even allowed inside the house.

"My parents are at their timeshare in Panama City." Sally said as she walked me upstairs to show me the rest of her house.

No parents. I had just assumed there would be parents. Especially since Daisy, who was also sleeping over, was dating Sally's brother.

"Daisy is going to sleep in my brother's room. My boyfriend used to sleep in my room too but we broke up so you can sleep in there with me instead."

"Ok, cool." I said, maintaining my chill-ness.

"Do you need to shower before we go to the game?" Sally asked.

"Oh, no, I showered this morning before school." I said, hesitantly. *Was that the right answer? Should I need to shower again?* I thought.

"Yeah, me too. But I need to shower again. I feel so gross after being in that nasty school all day."

Dammit. Two showers a day sounds much cooler. I'm so nasty.

Sally proceeded to get naked right in front of us. The conversation carried on like nothing was happening. Daisy was telling a story about how her boyfriend (who, again, was also Sally's brother) was a total asshole and why they were currently fighting. Sally motioned for us to follow her into the bathroom so we could continue talking as she showered. As Daisy proceeded to talk about her love troubles she, too, began to strip down to her Victoria's Secret matching underwear to change out of her "nasty school clothes". I never felt more repulsive in my life. I didn't bring extra clothes and I didn't shower. How stupid of me to think the clothes we wore to school would also be appropriate for spectating a baseball game.

After witnessing Sally's perfectly-thin and evenly-tanned nude body, I began a panicked calculation in my head of how long it would be before I had to reciprocate with my own nudity. At what point would I have to strip down in front of them in order to prove I am a normal girl? It would be creepy to always see my friends naked but they never see me naked. They would know I was hiding something.

My body wasn't the kind of body that nudity could be sprung upon. I often didn't shave my legs unless I had to. I wore boy short bikini bottoms because I could never quite figure out what to do with my pubic hair that didn't result in a blazing, burning red rash. My boobs were lovingly referred to as "ant bites" by my family, I wore push-up bras that were 90% push and 10% bra to give the illusion of actual breasts. I now knew that to be friends with these girls meant to live in fear that one day they would have to see me naked.

"I love your shower. I love taking showers with your brother in it. It's so sexy." Daisy said.

My attention now goes to Sally's rich-ass double-headed shower that she apparently shared with her brother. I thought of how odd it was that the parents installed a two-headed shower in their childrens' joint bathroom. How long did they expect these kids would shower together? This is still something I ponder regularly.

"Oh my god I know! I used to love having sex with my boyfriend in this shower. That removable shower head… Ooo! Tha bomb."

I snapped out of pondering the thought process behind her parents installing a *two-headed shower* in their *teen son and daughter's joint bathroom* to realize there was a silence where I was supposed to be talking.

"Oh, yeah. Uh huh. Sex in the shower. Right."

I had already had sex at this point, with an actual boy, but I was not used to discussing it. I was much more used to hiding it, denying it, or covering it up. I learned that apparently normal girls *like* talking about sex. And judging how long that conversation continued on, they liked talking about sex *a lot*. It didn't matter if they were having sex with your brother, all sex talk was on the table. Actually, the only taboo way to talk about sex was the way I did it… which was not at all.

"I know you and Josh had sex. How is it? Is he 'big'?" Daisy looked at me with wide eyes and her hands spaced out, moving them further apart and closer together, as if she was trying to guess the size of my boyfriend's member.

"Um… I don't know. I guess. I don't really…" I just trailed off. I physically didn't know how to make myself finish that sentence.

From that point forward in the sleepover, I was more of a tagalong. I didn't have sexy matching underwear. I didn't change clothes after school. I didn't know how to talk about sex. And at bedtime, when we all brushed our teeth together (as apparently normal girls do), I brushed over my retainer/fake teeth as if they were normal teeth. There was no way I was letting them know my teeth were removable.

The cool girls called my bluff. That was the beginning and end of my normal girl sleepover career. I just couldn't pull it off.

24

TRICHOTILLOMANIA

There I sat, in the Walgreen's parking lot, reading the instructions on how to apply false eyelashes.

It started as a slight itch which turned into a subtle ick. A hair felt out of place or just generally "wrong". Without consulting with my conscious brain, my subconscious sent my fingers on a hunt for the culprit. I knew it the moment I felt it, it was almost painful to touch. But the kind of pain I couldn't stop poking at. Like when you have a bruise that you can't quit testing to see if it still hurts. This "wrong" hair must be removed. It mocked me with its presence. Removing it became more important than anything else.

One time I rear ended someone because I was distracted looking for the hair that needed to be plucked. When I finally had it in my grasp - *Pluck!* Phew. Relief. Silence. Then, way too soon after, a new subtle itch began again.

Trichotillomania is the fancy (and incredibly terrifying-sounding) word for compulsive hair pulling. I began struggling with it when I was really little. It always got worse with stress. I once heard on *The Huberman Lab Podcast* that shame is an essential part of compulsive disorders like trichotillomania and I could see that in my own experience. The amount of time I spent hiding it, finding places to do it, covering it up, worrying people would find out, worrying people could tell, was so time consuming, and all of that was because of shame.

And that's how I ended up in the Walgreen's parking lot in the summer after 11th grade with a box of false eyelashes. I pulled one too many eyelashes out and I had to get a pair of falsies to hide the crime. I had never worn false eyelashes in my life and was barely capable of putting mascara on without getting flustered, so failure was very much an option.

With nothing but my tiny Cutlass Ciera rear view mirror to guide me, I attempted to put them on in the parking lot. For some reason the eyelash company decided to make the glue black, which did not seem like the wisest choice. I guess the assumption was that, if the user made zero mistakes, it would resemble eyeliner. But that was one assumption too far for me. By the end of it, glue was everywhere and the lashes looked like they belonged on an exotic dancer. And because all of this was happening dangerously close to my eyeballs, I had watery bloodshot eyes from the many, many times I got glue in them. I decided it was best to just do the fake lashes on the one bald eyelid and leave my other good eyelid alone. I'm sure that looked much better, and nothing like the creepy guy from *Clockwork Orange*.

I was putting myself through this debacle because I had a date with a boy I liked and I didn't want to cancel due to lack of eyelashes. So I slapped on the one furry caterpillar as best I could and headed over to his house. My plan was to stay to his left (since baldie was on my left). Unfortunately, he was very into me, in spite of my one furry eyelid. It wasn't long before he made a move. As soon as we started kissing I could feel the one lash smushed into my face and inch-worming its way up my forehead. I quickly made an excuse to go to the bathroom, hoping the dim lighting hid my secret.

I got to the bathroom and half of the lash was now vertical up my eyelid. The situation was not repairable. I ripped the caterpillar off, hid it in some tissue like the dead bug that it was, and flushed it down the toilet. I went back out, sat on the couch, and immediately started making out with him again just to keep him from looking at me as much as possible.

He never said anything to me about it, but we also never went on another date after that. I have always wondered what the heck he was thinking that night. Did he see my eyelashes evolve over the course of the evening? What possible explanation did he come up with, if so? Bless his heart, if he's still out there wondering I hope he stumbles on this book and finally knows the real truth. I wasn't insane... I just had a lot going on.

25

OPRAH SAYS I'M A PEDO

One day I was watching Oprah afterschool, when she had a special on catching pedophiles. I immediately perked up, because pedophiles were the worst thing on the planet in my eyes. So, if there was any way to help catch one, I was all for it.

"Dr. Expert, what are some warning signs that someone might be a pedophile that we can look out for?" Oprah asked. I leaned in, ready to learn.

"Well, Oprah, pedophiles will often do things that involve spending time with children. They are usually eager to babysit for you or volunteer to be the little league coach, things like that."

Hmmm... I thought, *I babysit. That's interesting. Am I "eager" to babysit? I'm not sure. I do enjoy kids. But does that mean I'm eager to spend time with them? I don't know. Anyway... go on Dr. Expert....*

"Many people imagine a pedophile to be a creepy, scary guy you would know to avoid. But that's usually not the case. A pedophile is usually someone who is very trustworthy and likable. They gain your trust so that you will feel comfortable leaving them alone with your children. But it is all part of the grooming process and the primary goal is to form a secret relationship with your child."

People are always telling me how likable I am. Am I pretending to be likable to be alone with kids? So many people trust me to be alone with their kids. Is that why I'm nice to them? Am I grooming?!

"Another important thing to know about pedophiles is they were often victims of sexual abuse themselves when they were younger."

And there we had it. That was all I needed to hear. *Shit. I'm a fucking pedophile. I just haven't molested any kids yet. Oh my god.*

After that, I did everything I could to not be alone with children, which was pretty hard since a lot of people wanted me to babysit for them because I was so freaking good with kids. However, I was terrified that the only reason I was so good with those kids was because I was accidentally grooming them and one day I would not be able to resist molesting them. It was all just a matter of time.

Forget the fact that the last thing I wanted to do on this earth was molest a kid. Forget the fact that I also went through this same compulsive fear of being a serial killer, which I never became. I was totally consumed by it. Every time I changed a diaper I asked myself *Did you look at their private parts for too long? Did you want to touch them? Do you find them attractive?* Granted the answers were always a resounding "NO" but it didn't stop me from asking again at the next diaper change.

It wasn't until I was older that I learned about something called Pure-O. It's a type of OCD where the compulsions are internal (in your head). I really could have used that awareness after Scott Peterson killed his pregnant wife Laci. I was fully convinced for about a year that I was a sociopath who didn't feel any real feelings which would one day cause me to lead a double life and I would inevitably have to murder my spouse if he ever tried to expose it.

26

MISUNDERSTANDINGS

I may not have been a natural with girls when I was a teenager, but the boys were a whole different story. The boys loved me. And I loved their attention. Since I was an expert at internalizing all of my negative feelings and knew how to be incredibly agreeable, to them I was a "chill girl". Also, thanks to years of avoiding femininity in order to not be accused of flirting with Larry, I was also considered a "low maintenance girl" too.

In addition to being chill and low maintenance, I used my trauma-born empathic abilities to detect boys' emotional wounds without them ever having to articulate them. I would then serve as a salve for those wounds with my bottomless compassion and nurturing presence. I was the Saver of Men. I was good at it and I was proud of it.

There was only one downside to being the Saver of Men. It could be confusing at times. I often didn't understand their way of communicating and therefore would end up in a lot of, what I liked to call, "misunderstandings".

Misunderstanding #1
In 10th grade I told a guy I needed some space. But apparently, to

him, "space" meant I wanted him to make more dramatic declarations of his love for me. He went to Daddy's grave, played him my favorite song on his guitar (which, by the way, was actually *his* favorite song but, whatever), and then proceeded to come to my house and tell me all of this. Not only that, but he said Daddy spoke to him and told him he wanted us to be together. This unannounced visit was after several pleads for him to please stop showing up at my house unannounced.

Misunderstanding #2

I broke up with a guy in the 11th grade. He took that to mean I needed him to watch over me from afar. So he followed me wherever I went and spied on my every move, and when I spent time with any other guys he popped up out of nowhere and threatened to kill himself.

Misunderstanding #3

The summer between high school and college I went to a party and got drunk. I misunderstood that, for guys, that meant when I passed out I gave them consent to pass my body around and use it however they want. Not fighting them equaled consent, even if the reason I wasn't fighting them was because I was unconscious.

Misunderstanding #4

During my first week in college I invited a guy I had met at a Freshman welcome event to my dorm room to listen to music and make out. I didn't realize that if you said yes to making out, you also said yes to anything else he wanted to do with your body. I told him I wasn't ready to do more yet, but he went ahead and did more anyway because I was apparently cruel if I left him with "blue balls". All that's on me for misunderstanding how much I was leading him on by inviting him into my dorm room in the first place.

Misunderstanding #5

When I was home during a college break, I misunderstood that if I had ever dated someone in the past, I was consenting to having sex with him any time he wanted to in the future. My "not tonight" didn't count because I had previously said yes on other nights.

I dealt with all of these misunderstandings, the last three of which were all within less than a year, by simply pretending they didn't happen. If I wished they hadn't happened, why not just pretend they didn't? I used them as a learning opportunity. I learned I was a stupid girl who made stupid decisions and put herself in obviously dangerous situations and exactly what I deserved.

27

COLLEGE READY

"She stole my shower shoes!"

"Cindy, did you steal her shower shoes?"

The RA was trying her best to navigate a conflict between me and my dorm roommate.

"No." I said.

I was lying.

First of all, it's worth noting my roommate had an epic pair of shower shoes. They were black and white Adidas slides that had a nubby footbed that massaged my feet when I walked. Second, I was not properly prepared for the communal shower experience since practically no one in my family knew anything about living in a college dorm. I had no idea how essential shower shoes would be and how often I would hear people say that people without them are either "disgusting" or "perverts".

"Oh my god she's lying! She's a psycho!" my roommate cried.

"Ok, let's calm down. Are you sure you didn't just *misplace* them?" asked the RA, who was clearly in over her head.

"No. I specifically put them in that spot because I wanted to see if she moved them… I *knew* she was taking them! Oh my god you don't believe me!" She started sobbing.

"Cindy?"

"I don't know what she's talking about. I'm sorry."

The truth was, I thought if I could just shower while she was in class, dry the shoes off, and return them to their rightful spot by her bed, this whole ruse would go unnoticed until the next trip home when I could get some damn shower shoes of my own. But alas, I wasn't great at remembering things or putting things back where I found them so that plan was pretty futile from the start.

"Oh my god she's lying! I am *not* staying in this dorm room with her. I do not feel safe with that psycho. You have to kick her out. She's a clepto!"

"Let's all just take a breath. I honestly don't think we can ask her to leave. There's no proof she did what you're saying she did and you have the shoes. Let's all just try to start over, ok?"

"Ok." I said.

My roomie got up and stormed out, her wailing slowly faded as she ran down the hall.

Unfortunately, my roommate wasn't believed because she was emotional and I wasn't. I had a lot of experience at lying both to myself and others. I knew that *calm* beat *hysterical* every time. Plus, no one would ever think someone would actually steal another person's shower shoes. Poor girl, I hate that I had to be her first college experience. I'm sure she was imagining braiding each other's hair and late-night gossip sessions and instead she got stolen shower shoes and her first lesson in the injustices of being a "hysterical woman".

She went home that weekend and never came back. My Inside World now had its own dorm room to come out and play in. Unfortunately, I had tucked away so many dark things into my Inside World by that point that it wasn't so magical anymore. What used to be a vast, colorful expression of imagination, now looked a lot more like an abandoned Denny's parking lot at 3am in the sketchy part of town.

28

HOW TO SUCCEED AT DEPRESSION WITHOUT REALLY TRYING

Step One: Get rid of the evidence.

I had all of my mail forwarded to my dorm address, instead of going home. That way any news of failing grades or dropped classes could remain my little secret. Considering both my academic and disability scholarship were dependent on my GPA, I wasn't sure what the long-term plan was for my little secret. But depressed people aren't really known for making long-term plans… we just kinda figure we'll be dead by then.

Step Two: Always answer the phone.

Little Mama called me every morning to wake me up for class. She knew from my high school years that no alarm clock on earth could summon me into an awakened state. Unfortunately, neither could her phone calls. I knew not answering her calls would cause suspicion or alarm. So I got really good at sounding really awake at 9am when my ringer jolted me out of a slumber that had just started a couple hours prior. I would clear my throat really really well and add about 5 decibels of cheer to my actual voice, shouting a few practice "Hello!"s before answering so it wouldn't sound like these were the first words I had spoken that day. Then, as soon as we hung up, I'd fall back asleep.

Step Three: Get really comfortable with lying.

I lied to the RA when she was sent to do a wellness check on me. I lied to friends about plans with other fictitious friends to cover up the fact that I was really lying in bed all those times they came knocking at my door. I lied to my family about all of the things I was learning in all of the classes I was never going to.

Those steps bought me a few months of unchecked depression, which gave me free reign to hate myself as much as I wanted and no one could stop me. And I hated myself a *lot*. I hated how I looked, I hated my personality, I hated the fact that I was a shitty depressed person and couldn't just get my ass out of bed. I felt like the single worst person on campus because everyone else got up and did college things. They were all capable of it and I wasn't.

This was so far from what I imagined my college experience would be. Much like when I moved in with Little Mama, it was another fresh start. A chance to reinvent myself. It went great at first. I made a lot of friends really quickly because, I hate to brag but, I'm pretty darn likable. In the first week I went to a Black fraternity stepping performance and to a Freshman roller skating event. I went to the gym and worked out, entered a twerking contest at a frat house, and frequented the campus cafeteria to socialize and eat the most delicious stir-fry I had ever had (ok, let's be honest, it was the *only* stir-fry I had ever had... stir-fry wasn't a common thing in Manchester).

But what I hadn't acknowledged was all of the traumas that had peppered all of those experiences. I still hadn't told anyone about any of my "misunderstandings" with guys. Before too long, my days began to play on repeat. Wake up to existential dread and promise myself to be a better human - Try to go to class but fail - Stir fry at the cafeteria - Visit friends and make plans for that evening - Party with friends and make out with guys - Come home drunk, order Papa Johns breadsticks for dinner, pass out - Wake up to existential dread - Fail to go to class - Stir fry in my room - Party with friends, make out with guys - Drunk - Papa Johns and pass out - Wake up to dread and self hatred - Skip lunch - Party with randos - Papa Johns - Wake up at 2pm numb - Avoid friends - Pass out at 6am - Repeat forever.

I didn't know anyone else like me. No one else I knew never left their dorm room. No one else I knew stayed up all night in existential dread. No one else I knew never went to class. Everyone else seemed to be having the college experience promised on the brochure. Why couldn't I do it too?

29

BABY'S FIRST INPATIENT

"I can't take it anymore. I love you. I'm sorry. Goodbye." I hung up on Little Mama.

My depression finally caught up to me. Thanks to a suicide threat I made from my car in an undisclosed location, followed by disappearing for several hours, I landed myself in my first stint in an inpatient mental hospital at the ripe old age of 18. My suicide threat wasn't a bluff. I wasn't just trying to get out of whatever lie I had been caught in by Little Mama, like she thought. That was just what sent me over the edge. I really did want to die. I drove around for hours trying to figure out what I could crash into that would definitely kill me but not hurt anyone else. A bridge seemed obvious, but they all had concrete barriers and I wasn't a stunt driver. I looked for a good tree to drive into but they all belonged in someone's yard and I didn't want them to forever have that memory associated with their tree. I couldn't even figure out a way to die without failing.

I was sent to the adult unit even though I was barely an adult. They took my shoelaces and replaced them with grippy socks and exchanged my clothes for a hospital gown. Let the healing begin.

The staff at the hospital were oddly friendly with the patients, like a little *too* friendly. They gossiped with us and some of the staff even flirted with the attractive patients. They asked us deeply personal questions but not as a therapeutic group, more like out of invasive interest in our crazy lives. We were their entertainment to make the hours of their monotonous day pass faster.

One day, the AA group leader pulled me aside.

"Why did you come to the meeting today?" he asked.

"I was just curious." I replied. There were no phones allowed and I was stuck in a hospital all day, required to go to a certain number of meetings. I was sick of all the crying in the normal therapy groups so I decided to change things up a bit and see what the AA crowd was like. I guess that was a mistake.

"I know you do drugs. Your mom said you're dating Black guys. Are you trying to tell me you date Black guys and you don't do drugs?"

I thought that was a pretty weird thing to say and I had a lot of questions. What was even weirder was he himself was Black. I reaffirmed once again that I wasn't doing drugs and, once again, it made no difference.

I still wasn't lying about not doing drugs, just like I wasn't when Dr. Desai accused me in high school. And I wasn't even dating Black guys. I had pictures of DMX and Nelly taped to my mirror in my dorm. After I was admitted into the hospital, Little Mama had to go to my dorm room to withdraw me from school and pack up my things. I guess she saw the pictures and made a few assumptions. I always wondered if she thought those were pictures of guys I was dating or if she thought I was dating Black guys because I had pictures of DMX and Nelly.

Most of the other patients were in their 30s and 40s. There was a mom/nurse who stole painkillers from her patients. There was a schizophrenic guy who was always talking about a wife that worshiped him whom we never saw and were pretty sure didn't exist. There was a guy who tried to stab someone in a psychotic episode. We all just hung out and swapped stories, ate terrible food, and waited until our insurance ran out or we convinced our caseworker we were no longer a threat to ourselves or others.

The painkiller lady told a story in group therapy about how much pain her patient was in as a result of her stealing her pain pills. *What a piece of shit,* I thought. But her story didn't make me feel like I was less of a piece of shit compared to her. In fact, it magnified my self-hatred. I felt like the worst person in the world and belonged right where I was, amongst people who committed elder abuse, attempted murder and abandoned their children. I assumed if I were already this screwed up at 18, by my 30s and 40s I would be 10x worse than those people.

It's funny how shame works that way. No matter how bad someone else was, I was always worse. I was actually jealous of the painkiller lady in a strange way. At least she could blame the drugs. I never had anything to blame but myself.

I learned two things by the time I discharged from my inpatient experience:

That the problem was me.

That it would probably always be me.

30

YOU CAN'T QUIT THE MILITARY

"I need you to make a plan for what you're going to do next." Little Mama said while sitting on the couch with her arms crossed in concern. A few days had passed since I returned home from the mental hospital. "I can't keep letting you live here and, now that you've lost all of your scholarships, I can't afford another college attempt."

I had already been thinking about it and only really saw one option. I was too fucked up for normal life. I needed something harsh to whip me into shape.

"I have a plan. I'm going to join the military."

She looked surprised. "I think that's a great idea. You need structure and discipline, somewhere you can't just lay in bed all day, wasting your life away."

Yes, I thought, *her seal of approval solidifies it. This is going to be the thing that fixes me.*

I'm not sure why it didn't occur to me, or any of the people who loved me or any of the mental health professionals I saw, that perhaps the military was not the best next step for a depressed, traumatized, eighteen year old who was straight outta hospitalization. At the same time, no one knew the full extent of my trauma. Plus the understanding of mental illness back then was different. Back in the early 2000s, the largest measure of a child's mental health was based on their external achievements, not their internal experience. Hell, no one even knew what an internal experience was. Therefore, it was logical for everyone to think getting me into the military and achieving things would fix me. They'd just discipline the mental illness right out of me.

"So you want to join the Air Force, huh?" said my recruiter. He was a wiry, energetic little man who acted like he was on seven cups of coffee and someone was timing him with a stopwatch when he spoke. He had spent the last hour convincing me that all he cared about in the whole wide world was my future.

"Yes, but I am a little worried about basic training. Other than playing softball in high school, I really am not very athletic..." Not to mention I had barely left my bed over the last year.

"Oh don't worry about that. My wife is the laziest, most out of shape woman on the planet. She barely works out. If she can make it through basic training, anyone can! I guarantee you!"

"Oh, ok. That makes me feel better, thank you. The other thing I'm worried about is going to war. I don't think I could actually fight people. I have trouble returning the wrong food order."

"Oh, please," he chuckled, "we don't go to actual war anymore. We have computers that fight our wars for us now! They will end the next war with an email. Plus, you're joining the Air Force. We are the safest branch there is. We're the smart ones flying planes while everyone else is fighting. The dummy Army guys will do all the work for you even if it did happen... which it *won't*."

"Oh my gosh that makes me feel so much better. I guess those were my main concerns..."

"Oh that's nothing then! You have nothing to worry about. Now, one little thing, I saw on your application that you take Prozac."

I was prescribed Prozac at the hospital and this time I was actually taking it. "Yes, they gave it to me in the mental hospital. Is that a problem?"

He sucked his teeth and made a concerned face. I thought he might be concerned that I had just gotten out of a mental hospital a couple of months prior. Or maybe he was concerned that I was struggling with depression and that might not be the best time to join the military.

"Yeah, you see, you can't join if you're on antidepressants." he said.

"Oh, ok. So I'm not eligible?"

"Well… not if you're on antidepressants… but if you *weren't* on them…"

"Should I come off of them?"

"If you're serious about being in the military, you should. You wouldn't have to disclose it on the application if you just stopped taking them from now on. That stuff doesn't really do anything anyways, it's all a placebo. Then you wouldn't be lying and you'd be eligible to enlist right away."

"Ok. If I enlist today, when would basic training start?"

"Next basic training date is August 15th. If you signed today you could go then!"

"Oh, wow, that's in two weeks. I would miss my niece's birthday party."

"You might as well get used to missing a lot of things if you're joining the military. Come on, it will be the adventure of a lifetime!"

I signed the papers and stopped taking the Prozac immediately. Two weeks later I was flying to San Antonio to start basic training. Boarding the plane in Atlanta, I felt so grown up. I was checking in by myself and the flight attendant gave me peanuts and a little drink, all paid for by the US government. *Look at me,* I thought, *I'm off to do something amazing with my life. It's all finally falling together.*

When I landed in San Antonio, the first thing to greet me off the plane was the intense booming screams of my drill sergeant. He was a lot less bubbly than my recruiter. The officers herded us away from the civilians exiting the plane and into our new normal. It wasn't quite as adventurous as I was expecting. It just felt scary. I found out later recruiters have a quota to meet and times had been tough for military enlistment since Don't Ask, Don't Tell.

The basic training scene was exactly like the movies and also completely different. Yes, it was a ton of yelling and belittling, standing in lines, and neatly made beds. What you don't see in the movies is male drill sergeants with female recruits. I didn't get to experience a female drill sergeant, but it seemed like the comments about our appearance and bodies would not have been as common with a woman. He commented on where our bodies were "fat", how beautiful or ugly our faces were, and whether or not men would want to fuck us. He had favorites and least favorites. I was a least favorite, of freaking course. I think it was because I was weak and looked scared shitless most of the time. His favorites all seemed to somehow enjoy the torture.

Most of the women in my barracks were lesbians. But they lied about it because, like I said before, it was the era of Don't Ask, Don't Tell. Later, when one recruit decided she'd had enough of basic training, she told our sergeant that she was a lesbian and she was promptly sent home. I never wanted to be a lesbian so bad in my entire life.

I did the very best I could to do well at basic training. I did my best to drink the two cups of syrupy orange electrolyte drink they gave us at every ten-minute-long meal. I did my best to deal with having no say in what I ate ever. I did my best to run and work out until I puked and not complain about it. I did my best to make my bed perfectly with sharply tucked corners. And I did my best to hide the fact that I was terrified of the big open showers, constant fluorescent lighting, never having time by myself, and crying myself to sleep every night.

But it all started catching up to me. Once again, the hardness of it all seemed like something everyone else was prepared for and capable of but me.

One day I was standing in formation for a training.

"You had better not get out of this line so help me god. I don't care if you're dying, you stay in that line." the drill sergeant said.

I had to pee. No one else was leaving the line. I wasn't sure what exactly would happen if I left the line but I did not want to find out. *Why does no one else have to pee?* I wondered. *We all drink the same nasty liquid and giant canteens of water every day, how were our bladders not in sync?* I could feel my bladder overflowing. I considered stepping out of line and going to the bathroom.

No. I thought. *He said he didn't care if we were dying, we cannot leave the line.*

I squeezed my thighs together even tighter in hopes of buying myself some time. I leaned forward slightly to make a little more room for my bladder.

He said he doesn't care if we're dying, do not get out of formation. Having to pee is nowhere near as serious as dying. So should I pee my pants? I'm going to have to pee in the next 2 minutes tops. Which will make him happy? Peeing my pants or going to the bathroom?

Mother Nature made the decision for me and I peed my pants. I figured other girls were probably peeing their pants too. I followed his instructions, I didn't get out of the line no matter what.

He walked by and saw me with soaked fatigues all the way down to my ankles. He got an inch from my face and screamed, "What in the hell are you doing?! Did you piss your pants?! How fucking disrespectful! What the fuck is wrong with you?!"

"Sir... Sir..."

"Speak the fuck up, you filthy pig!"

"Yes, Drill Sargeant. You said not to leave the line, Drill Sergeant Sir."

"You fucking smartass. So you pissed all over yourself to be a smartass! Give me 20 pushups in your piss pants and maybe that will shut your smartass up."

I got down and started my pushups. *A smartass? Why would I pee my pants to be a smartass? I was trying to make him proud!* He could hear me sniffling and saw my tears falling onto the ground.

"Don't you dare fucking cry in front of me!" he walked away and turned his fury onto the rest of the group, which was worse than when he was screaming one inch from my face. "This is what I mean! You are all a bunch of weak, spoiled, smartass women!"

He told another recruit to take me back to the barracks so I could change my pants. I could hear him say "Disgusting!" as we walked away. I didn't say a word the entire walk.

"Hey, it's ok. I don't know what I would have done if I had to pee either," the other recruit said in an attempt to reassure me.

But all I could think was, *She didn't have to pee. Why did I have to pee and no one else did? Why didn't I know that was a reason to get out of the line when he specifically said don't leave the line, even if you're dying? Why did everyone else seem to understand what to do but me?*

I went into our barracks and changed into new pants. I looked in the mirror, shaking, and whispered *You can do this* to myself. I took a deep breath and went to meet my chaperone recruit to head back. When we hit the doorway of our barracks, my body shut down.

"I can't go back." I softly whimpered.

"No, it's ok. It'll be ok." she said, unsuccessfully trying to reassure me again.

"No I *can't*." And that's the last thing I remember. Next thing I know I was sitting in a hospital bed talking with a military doctor.

"You passed out." he said.

"Oh." I replied.

"You've asked me what happened two other times. You don't remember me telling you that already?"

105

"No."

"You've been saying some pretty intense things. You seem more lucid now. Do you remember some of the things you've been saying?"

"No. What did I say?"

He ignored my question. "Do you have any history of depression or being suicidal?"

I looked at him, confused. I wondered why I was being asked about mental illness if all I did was pass out. "Yes, I've been in a mental hospital and medicated for feeling suicidal before."

"Ok, when was that?" he asked.

"In May." I replied.

"Of what year?" he asked.

"This year." I replied.

"Three months ago? You were hospitalized three months ago? You weren't put on any medication then?"

"Yes. Prozac." I replied.

"When did you stop taking it?" he asked.

"A few weeks ago, when I enlisted." I replied.

"Did you stop it cold turkey?" he asked.

"Yes." I replied.

"Who told you to do that?" he asked.

"The recruiter."

He dropped his head and let out a sigh. He told me I would not be returning to the barracks. He let me know he was recommending a medical discharge because I was not stable enough to continue basic training. Somehow, I had even found a way to flunk out of the military.

Off I went to my 2nd inpatient in less than six months. Military inpatient was a lot like civilian inpatient, same revoked shoelaces and grippy socks. Only there it had a lot more PTSD.

One day while I was there, on the way back to our rooms from group therapy, we passed a room and saw several soldiers gathered around a TV. They were dead silent, except for some muddled speculation I couldn't quite make out. The TV screen was filled with billowing smoke. Someone from my therapy group asked what was going on and the nurse quickly herded us along the hallway and back into our rooms. It was the September 11th attacks. I guess they didn't want to tell the fragile nutjobs that terrorists flew planes into the World Trade Center for fear that we might hang ourselves with a bedsheet from the distress (something that actually happened while I was there).

A week or so later I received a medical discharge. I later discovered that the day I peed my pants I had suffered a minor stress-induced stroke. But regardless of the reasons I was sent home, the mood I returned home to was that of clear disappointment. It seemed there was no future I couldn't manage to screw up.

31

THIS LOVE IS MAKING ME UNCOMFORTABLE

"Your crazy ex destroyed my truck." said my new boyfriend, Brad. We started dating shortly after I returned home from the military. I was still living with Little Mama and trying to figure out what I was going to do next with my life.

"W-w-hat?" I stammered.

"Last night, I left my truck at Dusty's house and then went out with some other friends. I guess he went over to Dusty's to hang out and didn't expect to see my truck parked there. When he saw it, he destroyed it and left."

Living in a small town, you get used to the fact that your boyfriend and ex-boyfriend have incredibly great odds at crossing each other's paths at parties. Also at parties, you might see your cousin, boyfriend's ex-girlfriend, or sometimes even your high school teacher.

"How do you know it was him?"

"Because I was laying right there inside my truck. Dusty accidentally locked me out of his house so when I came back I didn't have anywhere to sleep. I was banging on the door but I guess he passed out pretty hard. I didn't want to drive back to my parent's house drunk so I slept in the back seat. I guess he didn't see me in there because of my tinted windows. He picked up a rock and just started smashing."

"Oh my god! Wait... so you were *inside* your truck when it happened? What did you do?" I asked.

"Nothing. He was probably on drugs and he was with a bunch of other dudes, bashing my truck in with a rock. If I said something there's no telling what they might've done to me!"

"Fair point. Well, what are you going to do to him now?"

"Nothing. I'll call my insurance company and report it to the police."

"What does that make you feel about me since I'm the one who caused this?"

"Nothing. You didn't cause this. He's insane. It doesn't have anything to do with you."

Nothing. I had never dated a guy before who did nothing. I had only dated guys who did lots of things, most of them chaotic or abusive. But chaotic and abusive felt much more comfortable than what I felt when he said he was going to do nothing. *How would I know he loved me if he wasn't in a blind jealous rage over me?* I thought. My ex had shown his love by scraping a sharp rock down the sides of his freshly candy painted truck. Granted, I would prefer he didn't express his love for me. But how would Brad prove that he loved me more than that psycho if he did nothing?

That wasn't the only time Brad did nothing in our relationship. He also did nothing to fix my problems. He did nothing to enable me. And he did nothing to constantly reassure me that he still loved me. He had such clear boundaries while being just as clear that adored me. It drove me *insane.* It drove me so insane, in fact, that I fell madly in love with him and followed him to Barnesville to try college once again. As we know from the sobbing on the shitty couch, college didn't work out in Barnesville but the relationship did. He was the kindest and most brutal thing that had ever happened to me. I wasn't going to let that disappear from my life.

32

MORNINGS WITH PTSD

Alarm clock sounds

Can I hit snooze again?

I looked at the alarm clock. 7:00am.

Dammit. No.

I could feel that guy in college pressed up against me in my dorm room. I could barely breathe, he was so heavy. His breath in my ear. His hand pressed against my leg, holding it open. I resisted but, in order to not be overdramatic, I eventually just gave in.

Is that happening right now?

I opened my eyes and saw I was in mine and Brad's apartment in Midtown Atlanta. We moved there when Brad was accepted at Georgia Tech to study Engineering. Three years had passed since that moment in my dorm room. I was now safe and sound. *It's not happening right now but it feels like it is. That's so weird.*

God I was such an idiot. Why did I let that happen? Why didn't I fight? What a coward. Just like I was when Pal used to get bullied by Mama. I've always been a coward. Ugh, what time is it?

I look at the clock. 7:03am.

I need to get out of bed. Why can't I just get out of bed? I'm going to just hoist myself up on the count of 3. Ready? 1.. 2... 3... Hoist!

I didn't move.

Ugh. I am such a lazy piece of shit. Brad gets out of bed every single morning on his own with no issues. He's already gone to class. Class. He's in college. I'm not. Because I'm a failure. Which is why I have to get my ass up and go to work, if I'm not going to go to college I have to at least go to work. Remember that job I had when we lived in Barnesville? On college attempt #2. At that restaurant. That guy was so sexist. He always said women weren't reliable. But maybe he was right. I'm not reliable. I remember when he fired me because my hand was in a cast and I couldn't carry the big food trays. Or maybe it was because I was always calling out sick like I do. Brad quit that job out of principle when he fired me. He's such a good guy. I wish he hadn't done that. I was just dragging him down with me. I'm probably still dragging him down now. I bet he'd be so much happier if he had ended up with someone else.

I looked at the clock again. 7:14am.

Fuck! If I don't get up in one minute I will be late. I can't be late. Then they'll know I'm a lazy piece of shit. What am I going to wear today? Everyone at work dresses better than me. I dress like I'm going to court to try and get out of a DUI. They dress actual nice. They all probably know I'm a fraud. Or worse... they don't. I can't be late. I can't let them find out I was a mistake to hire. Get your ass up... 3... 2... 1... Get up!

My body still didn't move. I looked at the clock. 7:18am.

There's no way I can get to work on time now. How long has it been since I called out? Three weeks. That's pretty close. God I suck. I can't just do the simplest things. If I'm going to call out twice in one month I'd better have a good excuse. Car trouble? No, that sounds like a poor person's problem, that will just reinforce that I'm not sophisticated enough to work there... which I'm not. Sick? Sure but that sounds the most fake. Someone died? No, then everyone will be nice to me when I come back and that only makes me feel like a bigger piece of shit. Godammit, I guess I have to go with sick. What kind of sick? Appendix? Flu? Food poisoning? Food poisoning. I'll say I have food poisoning. Hurry, let me call them now before anyone is there because I can't handle lying to an actual person. It's much easier to lie to an answering machine.

"Hi, guys," I said in my best sick voice of someone who'd been up all night puking… which actually wasn't that hard to do since I never slept more than a few hours every night, "I'm not going to be able to make it in. I've been up all night with an awful case of food poisoning. I'm never going to Tokyo Sun for sushi ever again. Haha. I'm so sorry. I'll see ya'll tomorrow." I hung up.

An immediate weight lifted off my shoulders. A surge of energy rushed my body.

Phew. Thank god. I don't have to go anywhere or do anything today. I can just exist.

The burden of shame immediately started lowering back down on my shoulders again. But at least I could lie there by myself and not have to be a piece of shit *and* go to work.

We'll try again tomorrow.

33

WHAT KIND OF PERSON LIES ABOUT AN ABORTION

I was sitting in mine and Brad's apartment in yet another shame spiral. Despite the spiral, I had reasonably gotten my shit together. Long gone were the days of desperate attempts to become an adult the "right" way. I had accepted becoming an adult the harder way, degreeless with nothing but my own merit as a hard worker to back me.

Surprisingly, I was actually pretty good at raw-dogging life with no accolades to my name. By 21 I had a better job than I had imagined possible for a college dropout. I was working as a Case Manager at a Chinese adoption agency, a job that usually required a college degree but because of my natural knack for research and talking to humans, I had been promoted to the position sans degree. Brad and I were now engaged and, aside from the kind of rockiness you'd expect from two people who are dating and evolving at the same time, we were fairly stable. Brad was still attending Georgia Tech and I was currently the main breadwinner, being the only one with a grown-up job. I had always dreamed of living in the city. We had a three level townhouse (with our own garage) and two bay windows to look out over the city skyline at night. (There's no way in hell a couple of broke ass

20-somethings could afford that place now.)

I felt safer than I ever had in my life. But all of that wasn't enough to shake the constant feeling of overwhelming shame. There was one lie I told during my self-destructive years that still haunted me. It loomed over me as evidence that I was a bad person no matter what I did. I couldn't allow myself to enjoy the beautiful life that was taking shape while knowing I hurt others in order to get it. I had to get this monster off my back or else I felt my chest might cave right in.

"Hello?" Pal answered the phone.

I swallowed my heart. "Hey. I have to tell you something." I was never one for chit chat. Whenever there was bad news or a hard conversation, I always got right to the point.

"Oh god. What is it?" she said.

"I lied to you about the abortion."

During the summer after my year of repeated "misunderstandings", between the failed college attempt and the failed military attempt, there was this guy who made it clear he wanted to date me. And by date me, I mean he wanted to have sex with me. I think he got word that I was an easy score after hearing how many guys I had "slept with" at that party where I "misunderstood" passing out meant passing me around. Anyway, this guy was flirting aggressively and wanted to come over to see me. At that time in my life, saying "No" seemed pretty pointless. I had learned repeatedly that if a guy wanted me, he could just have me and there wasn't much I could do about it. So I said yes, he could come over. But I told him I had recently had surgery to remove cysts on my ovaries (which was a total lie). I had a friend who had that surgery and I remembered she couldn't have sex for a certain number of days after. That was my way of setting a boundary since a simple "no" never sufficed. He came over, we made out, he left. I felt such relief.

Shortly after that, an ex boyfriend said he wanted to see me.

He clearly wanted to rekindle things and, based on my previous "misunderstanding" with him there was a high likelihood he wouldn't take no for an answer. So I pulled out my handy dandy "surgery due to cyst-ridden ovaries" lie. He declined coming to visit at all. I felt so free. My body could just rest for a while and no one could touch it.

Unfortunately, my ex-boyfriend's mom knew Pal. These freaking small towns where everyone knows everyone! She asked my sister how I've been doing since my surgery, and Pal was a bit confused. There was nothing worse than being caught in a lie. Well, actually, I suspect being lied to is probably worse.

"Why did you lie and say you had surgery? And don't play dumb. I already called Little Mama and asked how you're doing. I'm pretty sure she would have mentioned if you had surgery. I didn't rat you out, by the way. You're welcome." she said, rightfully pissed.

"I don't know."

"What is wrong with you?"

That question always split me like an axe through wood. Every minute of every day I wondered what was wrong with me. But I did my damndest to hide that from everyone else. So when someone saw behind the curtain, and saw that I was a fucked up freak, I would do anything to be anyone but who I was.

"I… I didn't lie. I had… an abortion."

Why couldn't I tell her I was a girl who's body had been tossed around so much that she just wanted a break? Why couldn't I tell her I was a girl who didn't know how to say no any time someone asked anything of me? Why couldn't I tell her that the thought of another guy on top of me, consensually or otherwise, made me want to die? Because shame made me believe that whatever I was, was the worst thing a person could be. I would rather be any fake version of me than let someone see the real me. Instead of telling Pal I was in pain, I told her I had an abortion.

"I don't believe you." she said.

"I swear. I didn't want him to know so I made up the story about cysts."

"Who took you to get it?"

I lied about that.

"What medication did they give you?"

I lied about that.

"Whatever. Just let me know if you ever need me. Bye." She hung up.

She never pressed me for answers, I assumed she knew I needed the lie more than she needed the truth. We never spoke about it again until that day in my apartment, 3 years later, when the shame became too heavy to carry.

"I'm so sorry I lied to you." I said, already in tears, "When I said I had that abortion... I don't know why I lied... I just -" I still wasn't able to tell her the whole truth about why I lied. I didn't want her to feel sorry for me, I just wanted to free myself of the burden and let her hate me like I deserved. I prayed she wouldn't ask me why.

"Hey. It's ok. I knew it wasn't true. It's ok. I'm not mad."

"Really? But I am a horrible person. Why do you not hate me?"

"You're not a horrible person. That's why I figured you had a good reason you just couldn't tell me what it was."

She was right, and I still couldn't.

To this day that remains the biggest regret of my life. When people claim to not have regrets, I think they're full of shit. Or maybe they just never lied to their amazing sister about having an abortion. Though it would take many years to truly shake shame off my back, that moment was the very beginning of laying that burden down.

34

MY TENSE WEDDING

"... and she had better not even *think* of speaking to me at the wedding," Pal asserted, as she hand-gestured sassily to emphasize her seriousness.

"I know, I have it all arranged," I said. "She is sitting on the groom's side for the ceremony and I have already sent out the seating chart for the reception. Ya'll will be on opposite ends of the room the entire day."

"And I'm sitting with you, right? I'm the maid of honor."

"Yes, you're definitely sitting with me. Don't worry."

"Ok. I feel better, thanks. I can't believe you still speak to that woman." She said, side-eyeing me in disgust.

"I know, I'm just not really the type to cut people off."

"Oh I know. You are Queen People Pleaser."

"I'm sorry about how awkward it is making things. It's just... she did help raise me and I can't ignore that. But don't worry, I'll make sure Little Mama stays far away from you."

Pal had not spoken to Little Mama in years. Things got weird with Little Mama for a few years while I was in my late teens and early twenties. Pal and I both were struggling with young adulthood and I think it was all too much for her to handle. She cut both of us off for different reasons. She felt she was doing what was best for her and we felt abandoned. She later extended an olive branch only to me after I got my shit together, often crediting Brad for "rescuing me". But she never extended anything to Pal. I'm sure it was painful for Pal to watch me re-establish a relationship with her. But it was too painful for me not to.

On the flip side, after Pal gave birth to my niece (when I was 16), she and Mama reconciled. Mama divorced Larry and helped take care of my niece while Pal was at work. Somewhere between the birth and the divorce, they were able to call a truce.

"Why am I sitting on the groom's side during the ceremony? I think I have been more of a mother of the bride than *she* has." Little Mama said.

"I know, but you're sitting with the bride and groom's parents at the reception." I replied.

"Ok, but I don't know why I can't just sit on the bride's side. We're not Kindergarteners. She's not going to get cooties if I sit on the same side as her. It doesn't bother me at all to see her. I haven't done anything to be ashamed of."

One thing that hadn't changed was Little Mama and Mama still hated one another. This would be the first time they would be in the same room since my high school graduation four years prior, which required the same juggling act. One saw me before the ceremony, the other saw me after. One took me out to lunch to celebrate, the other to dinner.

"Why is *she* sitting with the groom's parents at the reception? Am I not your mother? I'm pretty sure I remember giving birth to you." Mama said.

"I know. But you're sitting on the bride's side at the ceremony, right in the front. And you'll be the first to come in and see me in the bridal suite right before the wedding." I replied.

"I don't know why she gets to come in the bridal suite at all. I hate that I have to share my time with her. It feels so disrespectful, I am your *real* mother."

The juggle was part of every milestone I ever had; graduations, weddings, funerals, baby showers… every single one. When I think of major life events I think of one word: juggling. In fact, the whole reason I chose to get married in Vegas in the first place was because I had never been able to enjoy a single life event without worrying about mediating some feud. Less people meant less people to mediate between. I thought Vegas would dim the spotlight on the tension because nobody took Vegas weddings seriously. *No dad to walk you down the aisle? No big deal, it's Vegas! Your family all hates each other? No big deal, it's Vegas!* But, as always, it turned out Vegas was just like at home: trying to make everyone happy ended up making no one happy. In the end, everyone felt like they were sacrificing or they were slighted. I wondered if they ever thought about how much I was sacrificing or how slided I felt.

Photographer: "Ok, now let's get the bride's side of the family together for a photo."

35

POOPY PANTS

"Is Aunt Pal going to die?" my seven year old niece asked, with her head buried into the passenger seat, peeking through the headrest to look at me.

"No, sweetie, she's going to be ok. Don't worry." Pal answered, both mortified for me and sympathetic for her daughter.

I was in the backseat of my own car, Pal was driving us the rest of the way home. It was the only time I ever crapped my pants in front of someone. But, as much as I hate to admit it, it was not my first time crapping my pants.

I struggled with IBS (Irritable Bowel Syndrome) for most of my life. There wasn't a name for it at the time, at least not one I was aware of, so I just thought I was a huge girl-baby who didn't know how to do basic grown-up things like hold it.

I developed several rules for working around my IBS. Rule #1: Knowing what I could and couldn't eat. No spicy foods, that was freaking obvious. No fried foods, no new or unusual foods, no grass-fed beef, no sugary foods if it's in large amounts, absolutely no curry, nothing with gravy or creamy sauces, no heavy cream, no salads, no kale, and (I was now adding to the list from the backseat of my Prius) no pot roast. The only "safe" foods were croissants, bananas, fries (unless they were too greasy), sandwiches, chicken, and pasta (as long as the sauce wasn't too saucy).

Rule #2: Always know where the nearest bathroom is located. And by nearest, I mean within about a 5 minute warning. This made travel to other countries incredibly difficult. *Do they use diapers in France? I wondered. Do they simply not have anxiety in Italy? Why do other countries not need public bathrooms around every corner... or even at all!?*

It was bad enough to have a "sensitive stomach" (as I called it then), but in addition to that I had a phobia of people hearing me poop. I guess I didn't want anyone to know I had a digestive system at all. In high school I broke up with a guy one time because I had to poop and his home only had *one* bathroom and it had a curtain for a door. I told him I needed to leave immediately and he thought my suspicious behavior indicated I was cheating on him. *Yeah, I'm cheating with another guy, I* thought, *and his name is John.* He told me if I left, to never come back because our relationship was over. I chose the KFC bathroom a mile up the road over him and then promptly came back 20 minutes later with a "change of heart".

So anyway, there I was, full IBS episode in swing and my phobia of pooping in front of people realized. Pal, my niece, and I were on our way home from a visit with Mama. We met her for Mother's Day (around Mother's Day, I should say, as we made a point to never meet her on actual Mother's Day) to have lunch at Cracker Barrel. I ordered pot roast (without gravy just to be safe), green beans, and mashed potatoes. All were supposed to be on my safe list.

When the urgency hit, we were sailing down I-75/85 through downtown Atlanta. I had already learned the hard way that urban areas were not great places to stop for urgent bathroom situations. They all had "ask for the key" or "customers only" policies which didn't leave enough time for making it to the bathroom before things erupted (pun very much intended). Faced with an impossible decision, I pulled over on the side of the road.

"I think I'm going to be sick." I told Pal.

"Ok, go ahead and throw up. It's ok." she said.

What she didn't know was that the sickness was going to come out the other end.

Throw up, I thought, *I wish I had to throw up. Vomiters get so much empathy. I can vomit on the side of the road no problem. People would rush to my side to hold my hair back. But what I'm about to do would get no such response. If it comes out the other end everyone runs the other direction and thinks you're disgusting.*

"Will you drive the rest of the way home? Fast?" I still couldn't just admit that I had to take a shit. It was such a phobia that I couldn't even utter the words.

"Ok." Pal said, and quickly hopped in the driver's seat.

With 30 minutes until home, I knew this mission was in vain. She did her best to make it in time, but only about five minutes after she started driving the inevitable happened. I sat in my own filth in the backseat of my car and just prayed my sister and niece would ever speak to me again.

"Are you sure Aunt Pal isn't going to die?" my niece asked once more.

No, little one, my body is not dying but my dignity just did.

36

THE CRIPPLING WEIGHT OF MEDIOCRITY

Brad and I bought our first home together in 2005. That's the same year we got married in Vegas and he graduated from Georgia Tech. We were both fans of trying to grow up as quickly as possible. By 25 we were living like we were in our mid-thirties. At the time I attributed it to being mature for our age and when people asked if we were rushing things I said we had just sewn our wild oats younger than most. In reality, we were "mature" because of a ton of unspoken trauma and what we called "sowing our wild oats" would better be defined as years of pain and self-destruction.

We bought a home in the 'burbs in a town outside of Atlanta that boasted having "the best schools". Buying in the 'burbs meant a lot to us. It was our best chance at happiness. For our entire childhoods, we had lived in rural Georgia. So far during our adulthoods, we had lived in the city because it was the opposite of rural Georgia. Neither seemed to have the answers to our problems. So now the only option left was suburban life.

I just knew our happiness could be found amongst cul-de-sacs, ice cream trucks, and HOAs. The 'burbs were like a foreign land to me. As a child we drove to them to trick-or-treat. I wondered if the other kids knew they were living on a real-life movie set or if it just felt normal to them. I would hear stories about kids sneaking out of their windows to go to other kids' houses. At Mama's house the closest thing I had to neighbors my age was a family of 8 homeschool kids who all had weird names and talked about God a *lot*. It was far enough away that I had to ride my horse to get there and once I was there, all we did was play Bible-themed board games or help take care of her millions of little siblings.

Brad and I moved into our first home and it was perfect. A small 1500 square foot 2 bedroom house with an iron spiral staircase that led up to a loft. We had a community pool and, for the first time ever, were able to paint our walls any color we wanted. Of all the colors in the world I went with avocado green. I don't typically perform well when there are too many choices. There was a cherry blossom tree on the tenth of an acre backyard. It was perfect. We had achieved a real grown-up life, avocado green walls and all.

About a year into being real grown-ups, I began to feel restless. That was supposed to be the finish line, and every day it felt more and more like a dead end. I began to imagine my life on an endless loop. Wake up to the same person every morning, work the same job every day, come home every evening and eat the same sensible rotating meals, watch the same TV shows, and go to bed to start it all again. There was no need to change anything. I had climbed to the mountaintop and now I would just look at this view every single day for the rest of my freaking life.

In the hot pursuit of building a life like everyone else, I had accidentally built a life like everyone else. Worse than that, I had built a life like everyone else in their mid-thirties. I had skipped an entire decade of growth and experience. I figured that must have been the decade where the other girls made their lifelong friends. Because I had none. It also must have been the decade they dated and broke up with lots of guys and learned how to be independent. I needed Brad to go to the grocery store with me. I began to suspect it may have been the decade when they found out who they were.

If one was missing an identity and was looking elsewhere to find it, it wouldn't take long before they stumbled on mission trips. I saw pictures of people holding little Black and Brown babies, helping them build a church or a school, appearing to feel really good about themselves. *That's it,* I thought, *I need to see the world and experience third world poverty so I'll be more grateful for what I have. That's where I'll find myself and also find contentment in that repeating loop that is my life until I die.*

I researched organizations that did volunteer vacations and decided Africa was where I needed to go. It was the birthplace of humanity. And it had lots of starving babies. *You have to be a good person if you go to Africa to help the needy kids,* I assumed. I started raising funds for my trip and telling everyone who would listen about how I was going to go help the little African kids. I started collecting toys and imagining their needy little faces light up when I handed them out. *I'm about to have an interesting life and make myself into a good person.*

On the day my deposit for the trip was due, I decided to take a pregnancy test just in case. It was positive.

37

OCP (OBSESSIVE-COMPULSIVE-PREGNANT)

Whether or not I agreed with pregnancy, pregnancy agreed with me. I had practically no morning sickness, I had more energy than normal, my mood had never been so stable, and I didn't have any shooting nerve pain that most of my fellow baby-growers complained about. I only gained the weight the baby needed and never got puffy or swollen in the face, feet, or hands. It was enough to make any mother hate me.

Mentally, however, was a different story. My intrusive thoughts came back with a vengeance. They had taken some time off since the days of worrying about being a pedophile or a sociopath, in fact I didn't even remember that I used to have those fears. They had long since disappeared and only left me with the remnants (a faint, general belief that I was inexplicably but conclusively a bad person who had to work very, very hard at pretending to be a good person). But now the fear was back with a clear new fixation: Postpartum Psychosis.

Postpartum psychosis was the diagnosis given to women who purposefully hurt or killed their children. I diligently researched it in preparation for my baby's birth. I read that one of the first symptoms was thoughts of harming your child. So I checked my thoughts constantly. I checked to see if I felt "connected" or "disconnected" to the baby in my belly a hundred times a day. *But how would I know what connected felt like? How connected is connected enough? Would I recognize disconnected if I felt it? Does a disconnected person realize they are disconnected? Did Mama feel disconnected from us? Had she had those thoughts of harming us? Would that genetically predispose me to be disconnected from my child?*

It didn't help that people constantly talked about how babies could feel their mom's mood in the womb and how it influenced their baseline mood after they were born. I tried to keep soothing music playing all the time in hopes to drown out the swarm of anxious thoughts I was constantly having.

"Promise you won't forget about me when he's born," I said to Brad one day while we were watching TV.

"What do you mean?' he replied.

"Just promise. That you won't fall in love with him so much that you forget about me."

"I promise." he said as he rolled his eyes at my seemingly unnecessary request.

I made Brad promise not to forget about me because I was afraid my jealousy would cause me to want to harm the baby. I wondered, *Is that what Mama felt when she accused Pal of flirting with her husband? Could I feel like that too? What if he doesn't look like me? What if he doesn't get my green eyes? Will I be able to love and connect with someone that looks different from me?*

All of the research I did suggested Postpartum Psychosis symptoms began *after* the baby was born. So now I would just have to sit and wait and see if this genetic ticking time bomb was going to explode. Then one day, just as I had been dreading for nine months, my contractions started. It was time to go to the hospital.

"I can't do it." I said as I stood in the doorway of our bedroom, Brad a few steps ahead of me with the hospital bag I had packed and repacked a dozen times, just to make sure everything was there. "I can't do this." It felt just like the day I stood in the doorway in the Air Force after I changed my pee pants. I wondered if I was going to have another stroke. *No*, I remembered, *this is worse. I'm going to have a baby.*

Brad turned around and stared at me but didn't know what to say.

"What if this was all a mistake? What if I can't handle a child? I want to take it back! I want to erase it!" I bent over with my hands on my knees, sobbing. I leaned against the doorway in pain, unsure if it was the contractions or my heart breaking.

Brad walked over and knelt down with me. "You can do this. I know you can. What can I do?"

I didn't like that Brad was seeing me this vulnerable. The shitty brown couch crying was years in the past. In fact, I pretty much never cried now. I saw crying as a weakness. But I was so scared I couldn't stop the tears from flowing. I took a few deep breaths and assessed my options.

Place the kid up for adoption. (This one did not seem likely as Brad was pretty invested at this point.)

Go take a shower and try to calm down.

I opted for the shower. The warm water fell over me and ran down my belly. I looked at how it had grown. There was a living being in there.

I just have to not kill it. If I don't feel connected to him I'll just make myself pretend like I do. Just don't kill it. I can do that.

I came out of the shower, ready to go. But, first, I had to check with Brad one more time.

"Do you still promise not to love him more than you love me?" I asked Brad.

"I promise."

As we loaded me and the bag into the car I looked at our house. I knew I would be returning here with a new roommate. *I hope I don't hate him*, I thought. But even if I did, I was going to keep my promise. I would just suck it up and pretend to love him as best I could and I would not let myself hurt him.

And then I met Maddox Rome Robinson.

Lots of people have kids and most of them think they're a big deal. Nothing about my birth or the human I birthed was any more special than anyone else's. But to have all of my fears dissolve away the moment I looked into his eyes was nothing short of magic.

When they laid him on my chest I didn't know where he ended and I began. Never had I loved anything more or so purely or so instantly. I knew I would not only never harm this human, but I would burn cities to the ground to spare him an ounce of pain.

All of the trauma and grief I had endured up until that point in my life was worth it if it eventually led me to him. He was mine. He was of me.

Unconditional love is a precious thing. My life had allowed that feeling to be rare enough so that I would know the full weight of it when it was handed to me. Years have gone by since that day (fifteen to be exact) and my feelings for him are the exact same. I have neither felt entitled to his love nor gotten used to it. I know not every mother has the privilege of such an instant connection with their child. I can only imagine the sorrow and extra challenges that brings. But it is important to share *my* truth, which was that motherhood was never burdensome for me. In fact, it felt like being set free.

I thought it was going to be so hard to love my son. I thought it was going to feel like a constant struggle between his needs or mine. I thought it would be hard to resist yelling at, punishing, hitting, or critiquing him. To my merry surprise, not harming him would be the easiest thing in the whole world to do. I no longer worried about Brad loving him more than me. Loving him *was* loving me.

I knew the moment I met him that he was good. He wasn't just good. He was the brightest ball of light I had ever seen. The day he was born I learned I was capable of creating something so bright.

38

NOT ME

It was abundantly clear upon meeting Maddox I was willing to do whatever it took to give him a better childhood than I had. There was only one problem: I only knew what a good childhood *didn't* look like. I knew not to believe he was out to get me. I knew not to accuse him of flirting with adults. I knew not to make him regulate my mood. And I knew not to abandon him when he was difficult to love. I knew I couldn't just *not* do those things. I would have to replace the bad childhood things with good childhood things. But I didn't know what to replace all of that with. What made a childhood good?

After he was born, I left my job at the Chinese adoption agency to begin working at his preschool. It was a move down on the career ladder, but we had a state-funded daycare budget on private preschool ambitions. So I utilized the clout I built from working my way up to a Case Manager position at the adoption agency to get a job at the fanciest preschool I could find. They let their employee's children attend for free. Maybe we couldn't provide our son with fancy rich parents but we could at least provide him with fancy rich friends.

I had a wealth of parents (pun intended) I could observe at the private preschool to help me navigate the whole good parenting thing. There were the parents who came in frazzled when they dropped their child off. They were almost always running late and their child was usually still wearing an overnight diaper from the night before. There were the parents who should probably be divorced, that gossiped to us about one another behind each other's backs. There were the parents that cried more than their baby did at drop off who stood outside the window for an hour before finally leaving, continuously popping back in to "comfort" their child, thus starting their child's separation anxiety all over again. But these were just more parents showing me the kind of parent I *didn't* want to be.

Then there were the parents who were punctual, friendly, had sweet babies that were dressed in clean, matching clothes every single day. *That is who I want to be like,* I thought, *They've got it all figured out.*

Watching their every move, I discovered those parents prioritized education over everything. They were really big on giving their children *options*. Options were the ultimate goal. If you could make the Olympics or Ivy League schools an option for your child, then they could do practically anything they wanted with their lives.

Ever so studiously, I began imitating those parents in order to give Maddox options too. I played classical music in his bedroom at night because they said it raised a child's IQ. I made his baby food from scratch because they said pesticides would stunt his brain development. I taught him sign language so he could start communicating his needs and emotions as early as possible. I replaced overstimulating light-up toys with wooden blocks and flash cards of US presidents. I did the cry-it-out method so he didn't become too coddled and not be able to make it in the cut-throat world. I didn't know if he would go to the Olympics or Harvard, but I sure as hell wasn't going to be the reason he didn't.

At every pediatrician's appointment I asked about his milestones and if he was ahead of target. And my pediatrician told me at every appointment that babies all develop differently. She said his current pace of meeting milestones had no bearing on what his future may hold, good or bad. But she wasn't parenting like her life depended on it. I needed to know I wasn't screwing this kid up *now*. I was trying to raise a child with no obstacles and zero trauma, while only knowing a childhood full of obstacles and traumas. I needed constant reassurance that I was doing it right. I didn't have time to wait until he was 18 or 25 or 45. I needed to know this week, this day, this minute.

What I was really trying to do was raise him to not be Me. I had so much guilt for giving him Me for a mom. What did I have to offer him? Mental illnesses and learning disorders? Brad was smart, resilient, and educated. He was revered by everyone as a hard-working, morally-strong human. I was a block of cement, dragging everyone down. Maybe if I did my job well enough he wouldn't have ADHD, OCD, or anxiety. His stomach wouldn't destroy itself every time someone was displeased with him and maybe he wouldn't hate himself. Maybe I could make up for being his mom by teaching him how to not be Me.

39

A CONVERSATION WITH MY THERAPIST

"Um, so you were raped…" my therapist said, as she looked up from her pencil and paper with a concerned look on her face. I was giving therapy another try, as an adult this time, to see if she could help make me a better mom for Maddox, who was now three years old.

"No no no, maybe I'm saying it wrong. Every single time I put myself in that position. I was drinking… *and* flirting. And that one guy I stopped cold turkey alone in my dorm room. Like, so I was a 'sort of yes' and then suddenly a 'no'? That's pretty confusing, I know. And the group of guys, that was awful, but I was passed out. So maybe they thought I was into it. I don't know how I was acting, maybe I was acting into it… "

"Yeah, all of that is rape."

"Oh, ok." I replied, my brain not quite sure where to put this information.

"A big step in trauma recovery is sharing your trauma with safe, loving people in your life."

"Sure. That's why I'm telling you."

"Actually, why you originally told me was because you were afraid you were making yourself sound too 'good' in our sessions. So you started confessing 'bad' things you had done in order to give me a clearer picture..."

"Oh, ok, well, ok, either way. So it was rape. Ok. And now I've told you." If it had not been too cartoonish I would have actually dusted my hands off to signify we were done with this topic. But instead I just stared at her blankly and hoped we would move on to the next subject.

"I would strongly suggest telling your husband or your sister, they are your most trusted people. I think they've proven to unconditionally love you."

"No. I could never. I didn't tell them for so many years because I thought it would make them look at me differently. But now, it's been so long, it seems like I'd just be doing it for attention. They know about the molestation. They already know I'm 'poor pitiful Cindy.'" I said with air quotes.

"It's not about you being pitiful or being felt sorry for. It's about you believing you're worthy of telling your whole story. It says something to your body when you hold onto shame around traumatic stories like these."

"Ok, but for now telling you is as far as I'm gonna go."

40

ATTEMPTING MOM FRIENDS

"Come on in! Sorry my house is a mess!" chirped Lisa (who's name has been changed to once again protect the normal). Lisa was one of a group of mom friends that I had made courtesy of Maddox. Maddox was a social butterfly in preschool, and thus always getting me invited on playdates. I had never even heard of a playdate until I moved to the 'burbs. The majority of the kids I played with growing up were my cousins, but when I did hang out with a friend, parents weren't involved. You'd get dropped off at someone's house (if they didn't live close enough to walk/bike to) and you wouldn't see an adult the entire time.

Parents were heavily involved with playdates in the 'burbs, especially moms. If I didn't perform well, Maddox would lose that friend. I no longer had to just worry if *I* had friends, now my kid was counting on me too.

On this particular day all the mom friends were going to chaperone the preschool's field trip to the zoo. I took the day off so I could join the group, which meant I took the day off to go on a field trip at the very same preschool where I worked. Lisa invited me to ride with her, so we could "pregame" the field trip. I had no idea what that meant.

Despite her apology, Lisa's house was not a mess. In fact, it was perfectly in order. Plus she had the most delicious scented candle burning that I had ever smelled in my life. Walking through her perfect house, I felt like I was learning from a master. I wished I had a notepad and pen.

Candles. Got it. I need to get candles. How did she know what candle to buy? That candle smells like financial security and unconditional love. What the hell is that glorious scent?! I'm going to Bath and Body Works tomorrow.

"What can I get you to drink?" she asked. "I have coffee, tea, soda, or water. Or if you want we could open a bottle. Do you prefer white wine, red wine, or prosecco?"

Offer guests something to drink when they arrive. That's so classy! I don't think I do that. And she has so many options. I really need to make sure I have more options. Right now in my fridge I have water and cranberry juice. Thank god we didn't pregame at my house! She even offered wine! Also, do people drink wine in the afternoon? That's so grown up! And what the hell is prosecco?!

Lisa wore a cute, in-style outfit with calf-length boots (in 2011 when calf-length boots had just hit the scene in a big way). She talked about her years as a recruiter before becoming a stay at home mom, a job that even after being told several times what it meant I still had no idea what it meant. She had limitless energy, perfectly styled hair, and smelled amazing. *She's just so... put together,* I thought.

She talked about her parents and her childhood with light-hearted fondness. When it was my turn to reciprocate, I wasn't sure what to say. I couldn't think of a single light-hearted, nonchalant thing about my childhood. All of my stories required a full backstory and were filled with plot twists and dark elements.

Wait a minute. Is Lisa who I would have been without the trauma? Just a person with a positive baseline mood? Would all of that extra energy not

138

spent on anxious thoughts and existential dread go to picking out candles and buying prosecco? Or knowing what prosecco even was?

Lisa wasn't alone. All the mom friends from the fancy preschool (where they all could afford to pay the tuition and didn't have to work there for the free tuition like me) just seemed to know things I didn't know. They talked about cheeses and could easily distinguish them by name alone ("It's a Gruyere" and everyone would say "Ooohh" as if they knew exactly what that meant). They had a wild or amazing story for pretty much any city or country you could think of. Meanwhile, the city I had the most knowledge of was Vegas, and that seemed like the one city no one was impressed by. I was embarrassed to admit the real reason I got married there was because, at the time, I thought it was the fanciest and most classy place I had ever seen.

Though I never formally requested a drink, Lisa served me Prosecco with a batch of homemade cheese straws (that I had to refrain from devouring to not look like a starved orphan). *Ok, so prosecco is just carbonated white wine... got it. How is that different from champagne?*

"Are you ready to head over to the field trip?" she asked me.

"Yeah, I'm excited to see them on their first little field trip."

"My god! Can you imagine? All the moms are hiding cocktails in our water bottles. How else will we survive wrangling twenty four-year-olds at the zoo??" Lisa laughed hysterically.

"Oh that's funny." I said. *Is she serious? She's not serious. It's a joke. Right?*

"What do you want to put in your bottle? I have pretty much everything in the liquor cabinet. I'm putting a vodka tonic in mine."

"Oh, uh. No, I'm ok. I work there, so... I probably shouldn't be seen drinking."

"Oh, right! Ok!" she pepped as she poured Absolut into her Yeti 32 oz cup.

Drinking always seemed important to my mom friends. I hated

drinking. But I learned in order to keep mom friends I would have to become comfortable with drinking. There was no faster way on this earth to weird someone out than to say "No, I don't drink, thanks." Instead I learned how to sip slowly and carry a drink around as a prop. Because the minute the glass was empty someone was always filling it up.

By the time we arrived at the Atlanta Zoo, the mom group was already tipsy. We were supposed to keep track of two kids each but I realized quickly I would be keeping track of all eight of our kids.

I went to take a bathroom break and Lisa followed me into the bathroom.

"Oh, it's a single bathroom," I said.

"Yeah I know. Let's go in together." she slipped in and immediately headed for the toilet to have a pee, slightly stumbling along the way.

Why do women love being naked around each other so much... I thought.

She finished up and it was my turn.

"Go ahead!" she said.

"No, I just wanted to wash my hands. The kids keep holding my hand and they're all so sticky." I said with an eye roll. She let out another massive laugh as she washed her hands alongside me.

"You're hilarious!"

We left the bathroom I held my pee in until we got home. I thought my bladder was going to explode.

41

DODGE THE SUBJECT

"I think I'm going to enroll in massage therapy school." I said confidently to Brad one lazy Sunday over breakfast.

"Oh really? That's great! One thing though… what about the fact that you generally don't like touching people?"

The next day in my therapist's office.

"I think I'm going to enroll in massage therapy school."

"Ok, awesome. Should we unpack first your trauma around being alone with men, while they will be naked? Do you think that might be triggering for you? And also, have you still not shared that trauma history with anyone?"

Later that week on the phone with Pal.

"I think I'm going to enroll in massage therapy school."

"Ok, cool. Is this because we just got that massage last weekend? Wasn't that your first massage ever? Are you sure you have enough experience with massage therapy to know you want to do it for a career?"

Everyone meant well, and everyone made valid points. Did I go ahead and do it anyway? Absolutely. Did they turn out to be right? Absolutely not.

I've made impulsive decisions that cost me greatly and I've made impulsive decisions that were the brave first step on long and fruitful journeys. And I can never tell the difference at the time I'm making them.

While massage therapy was a fairly new career option I was exploring, I had been feeling the itch of discontentment around my job for a while. Maddox was about to enter Pre-K, and we would no longer need the free tuition, which was the reason I started working at his preschool in the first place. I couldn't go back to the Chinese adoption agency I worked at before because China had closed all international adoptions indefinitely. Finding another leap-of-faith employer to hire me for a position above my education level based on my pure gumption was not likely to happen again. Especially since the last five years were spent changing diapers, that experience didn't translate over to many other professions. I was pushing 30 and still limited to the same jobs 18 year olds could get out of high school, and that was embarrassing.

I managed my embarrassment by dodging the subject of my formal education (or lack thereof) entirely. As soon as the topic of college came up in conversation ("So, where did you go to school?" - I freaking hated that question.), I suddenly had to pee or take an urgent call or trim the hedges, anything to get the hell up out of there. I thought if people found out I wasn't college educated, they would think less of me. And that's because they did. On multiple occasions throughout my life, my opinion was dismissed and replaced with the opinion of someone with letters after their name, even if those letters had nothing to do with the opinion they had. It's crazy how much people assume you aren't capable of if you weren't capable of finishing college. And vice versa.

When people did find out my dirty secret, they would try to console me by replying, "But you're so smart. You should go back and finish!" As if not finishing college automatically meant I was dumb. As if there was no other reason a person would not have a college degree.

I imagined if I answered them honestly: "Well, Susan, my entire childhood was steeped in trauma and learning disorders that I never got the proper treatment for. Instead, I was medicated and, if that didn't solve the problem, I was told I was lazy. Then, when I did try college, I was raped more than once on campus. So now the classroom triggered my learning disorder trauma and the campus triggered my sexual trauma, making it practically impossible to maintain the GPA I needed to keep my scholarships. (I always thought it was weird there was a GPA requirement to keep a disability scholarship. Like, isn't it possible my disability is the reason I can't meet the GPA requirement?!) Anyway, so then I couldn't afford college even if I was able to survive it. And by the time I *could* afford it *and* survive it, I was resentful that I had to. I had noticed over the years that I was just as valuable of an employee as anyone else with a degree. I couldn't imagine being a decade older than my classmates, going into debt, to learn things I had already learned on my own for free."

That was not an explanation I was ready to share at dinner parties. In fact, as my therapist so kindly and repeatedly pointed out, I still hadn't even shared my whole story with my husband.

The main thing hanging over my head was I didn't want Maddox to be ashamed of me when he grew up. So when I went to get that massage with Pal I couldn't stop thinking of what a nice work environment it would be. I loved how low sensory the darkened room was. I loved how little conversation took place. But most of all, I loved how much respect her profession seemed to command. She wasn't a "masseuse".

She was a *massage therapist*. She had knowledge about muscles and inflammation and could tell where I held my stress based on my body posture. I would be proud to say I was a massage therapist. I asked where she trained, and when I looked up the school and saw how hands-on the training was, I would be learning in a way that worked for me. In two years I could get a job that I could be proud to say out loud.

So I did it. I finished massage therapy school with perfect attendance and straight As. I continued on and got specializations in trauma touch therapy and pediatric massage. I didn't struggle and fail like I had so many times before. And I no longer had to dodge the subject of my profession or education. More than all of that, it was the turning point where I started to feel like an example to Maddox rather than a cautionary tale.

42

EXCUSE ME, SIR, I BELIEVE YOU'RE SITTING ON MY TRIGGER

"Hi, Sweetie! How was your day?" I greeted Maddox with a big smile as he climbed into the backseat at carpool pickup.

"Great!" he replied with his usual jolly disposition.

I always made sure to greet Maddox with a big smile for two reasons: my mommy issues and my daddy issues.

Mama's mood was unpredictable. Carpool time was one of my most nervous times of the day, waiting to see what mood she would be in so I would know what mood I could be in. I didn't want Maddox to have to wait nervously to see my face at carpool. So I made sure it was the same face every single day.

Losing Daddy so suddenly left me with the keen awareness that the ones you love could die when you least expect it. So now I expected death was around every corner. Every day when I dropped him off at school I thought it would be the last time I saw him. Every day he climbed back into my car after school was worth celebrating.

When we got home from our car ride of blasting wildly inappropriate music and singing at the tops of our lungs, I saw an email from his teacher:

Mrs. Robinson,

I wanted to follow up with you about Maddox getting in trouble today. He would not stop talking and was being disruptive in class despite repeated attempts to redirect him. Please sign the behavior form and return it to school tomorrow.

Sincerely,
  Mrs. Mitchell

I fumbled through his backpack for the behavior form. Nothing. I re-read the letter again, dissecting every word.

My initial reaction was, *Who the hell expects Kindergarteners not to talk in class? This teacher is going to break his spirit! Is talking really a legitimate reason for a five year old to get in trouble anyway?!*

Then I read it again, this time with a shame lens.

Why did he not tell me about this in the car? Does he even care or have remorse that he got into trouble? Oh God, he's going to be a liar and a problem child just like me.

I called him into the room for more clarity so I could decide which spiral to go down, the anger or the fear. As I prepared for how to have that conversation with him, I remembered something people always did when they confronted me about something (and I had a lot of experience at being confronted about stuff). They always tried to trick me by seeing how much I would confess first. They would say things like "Did anything happen at school today you want to tell me about?". I always hated that. No. Nothing about what happened at school today was ever something I wanted to talk to them or anyone else about. Facing my first opportunity on the other side of that coin, I decided I was going to do things differently.

"I just got an email from Mrs. Mitchell. She said you got in trouble

146

today. She said I'm supposed to fill out a form to send back tomorrow. But I don't see the form anywhere."

"I threw it away." he said, his eyes dropped down to the ground and his shoulders slumped, just like mine always did.

"Why did you throw it away?" I said, trying to remain curious and calm, but slowly coming apart at the seams on the inside.

"I didn't want you to see it. I thought if you didn't see it you would never know."

Oh my god. I thought, *He's sneaky and a liar just like me. At five years old! Is that normal?! Oh god. He got the bad person gene and he's doomed to be just like me: a failure at life who will live in shame and have to force himself to perform as a good person for the rest of his life...*

But he's my baby, the other half of my brain chimed in, *He's so sweet.*

Not for long. You'd better whip him into shape so he doesn't end up just like you. Scare the crap out of him. You cannot tolerate any lies. Maybe if someone had caught my manipulative ass sooner there would be some hope for me.

But I have a hard time believing that's what he needs right now. Oh, I don't know...

That's all part of the manipulation. He's just like me. Everyone thought I was so sweet and so kind and we all know now I was a fraud who was fooling everyone. He's a monster, just like me. Face it.

My brain was at war with itself. Over a piece of paper thrown away by a five-year-old. Meanwhile, he was staring at me waiting to see how I was going to respond. Then suddenly something dawned on me.

Wait. Did he just immediately confess? He admitted he threw it away and even told me why. I never did that. I always doubled down on my lies. Maybe I only lied because I didn't feel safe telling the truth. Maybe lying was my fear response, and when people don't feel as afraid they don't lie as much.

I looked in his eyes and, with the most clarity I had felt in a long time, I knew he was not a monster. In fact, it made me question whether or not I was actually a monster, either.

43

CULTURELESS

Ever since I moved out of rural Georgia, I either apologized for or hid from my Southern roots. I frequently made fun of Manchester in order to differentiate myself from it. I made fun of how much they loved guns, how stupid their accents sounded, and how ignorant they were about other cultures. And while there were reasons for me to question their intense passion for automatic weapons and lack of compassion for humans that were different from them, my motives were not always about social justice. They were mostly about a deep insecurity that to be Southern meant to be lesser than.

Urbanites loved to hear a reformed ruralite diss their roots. I obliged them with pleasure. They held the key to redemption from my embarrassing heritage. To gain acceptance into the *cultured* world, I ate at fusion restaurants (at which the owner rarely derived from either of the cultures they were fusing). I invaded Black-centered events, like African dance classes (desperately trying to prove that I was someone who could be "invited to the cookout"). I acted afraid of bugs, getting dirty, and being outside in the heat, all things that would be a dead giveaway that I was a country bumpkin. Everything natural I associated with redneck. Because of this self-urbanization, my Inside World slowly dwindled and my time in nature became limited to drinking IPAs on a rooftop patio.

Then, as Maddox became his own human, that little shit kept dragging me outside. The *real* outside. Into the heat. Into the rain. Into the cold. Into the mud. Into the rivers and streams and storm drains. He wanted to be outside all the time.

When we would go home to visit his grandparents he would come alive. He sparkled as Pawpaw (Brad's dad) showed him how to shoot a BB gun. After spending the majority of my adulthood refusing to allow a gun in our house and preaching anti-gun laws (as all good city-dwelling liberals do), my son was now a gun owner at the ripe old age of five. I avoided telling people he even called his grandfather "Pawpaw" because it sounded so… country. So *uncultured.*

And I was striving to be cultured. Super cultured. I was looking for culture wherever I could find it. I was looking for the *authentic* street tacos. I was fasting for Ramadan and attending Eid al-Fitr at a mosque to honor the beautiful Muslim religion. I was pretending to love and be able to pronounce Challah bread. I was trying to learn French on the off-chance that one day a random French person would be standing near me and I could blow them away with the fact that a person in the South spoke perfect French. *Très cultivé.*

But if someone asked me to prepare an authentic Southern recipe that had been passed down for generations in my own family (like dressing or banana pudding)… or attend a Baptist Church for Easter… or bake some buttermilk biscuits with homemade jam… or use my actual native Southern accent… I'd say *fuck no.* I was ashamed of it. I was looking for authentic culture anywhere but where it was authentic for me.

Maddox messed all that up. He made me the biggest hypocrite on the planet. I had spent years training the Southern out of me and now I had a kid who loved all of it. When he was 7 years old we could no longer deny that the 'burbs were gonna suck the life right out of him, and we had to admit they were sucking the life out of us too. We had to be closer to nature and set this little hick free.

We found a little double-wide trailer that had been renovated into a free-standing home. It had two porches that were almost the same square footage as the home itself. It all sat on 2 acres of land which was just enough to hold chickens and goats, a couple of cats, and a dog. And by returning him to the wild we were returned ourselves, too. As I saw him nourished by the sunlight that sliced through the trees, I remembered how much I loved sunbeams against my own face.

I worried that returning to my own culture meant returning to *all* of it, biases and fear-based mindsets included. But I realized I could speak French *and* I could sip sweet tea in a rocking chair on the front porch. I could spend all day making divinity and fudge at Christmas without being Christian. I could pass down gardening tips without passing down racist and anti-gay ideaology. I could embrace the heritage I was proud of, and create a new heritage at the same time.

44

YOU REALLY DO LOVE ME

It had been seven years since my therapist told me I needed to share my whole story with the ones I love. I was now 35 and saw no reason to take her advice. I was doing just fine and if something worked for 35 years, there was likely no reason to change it.

Then I saw the story about Brock Turner. He was a punk who sexually assaulted a woman behind a dumpster while she was unconscious and had to be intervened upon by a heroic bystander (a European, of course, as Americans tend to turn a blind eye). He was only sentenced to 6 months in jail because the judge didn't want "one mistake" to ruin his promising future (he was a student at Stanford on a swim scholarship). Much about the judge's sentencing was based on the assumption that because his victim was drunk and flirting with him at the bar earlier that evening, she probably would have consented to the sexual activity if she was still conscious. To my shock, there was outrage over the case. It was the beginning of #MeToo and for the first time I was seeing myself acknowledged as part of the movement.

Something about this cultural shift made me no longer feel comfortable in my secrecy. I now felt suffocated by it. One day, while mopping the floors, the discomfort overcame me. That discomfort sparked another brave wave of impulsivity. I picked up my phone and, before I could change my mind, told Brad and Pal my whole story.

"Hey. Sorry for sending such a heavy text while you're at work but it's this or nothing. I need to tell you something but I don't want to make a big deal about it. And if it makes you think differently of me, I totally understand. But when I was younger I was raped on three different occasions. I'll spare you the details. I just needed to let you know. I didn't say anything before because I didn't realize it was rape at the time and I was embarassed. Then once I realized it was rape so much time had passed I didn't want to seem like I just wanted attention. I'm sorry for lying to you. I will understand if you are angry with me. I love you."

Admittedly, a text wasn't ideal. In the middle of their work day, no less. But like I said, it was that or nothing. After hitting *SEND* I sat, my hands and insides shaking, waiting for a response.

Brad's Response: "I am so sorry, sweetie. Thank you so much for sharing that with me. Maybe we can sit down tonight and you can tell me anything you need to. Of course I am not angry with you. I'm so sorry you've had to go through this alone. If anything I feel closer to you now because I understand you so much more. I love you."

Pal's response: "Oh no I'm so sorry this happened and that you were afraid to tell me. Do you want to talk? I am here for you any time and of course I'm not angry. I love you."

After reading their texts, I finally understood why my therapist insisted that telling the people I loved would be part of my healing process. Every "I love you" I had received from them prior to that moment was meant for someone else. They *thought* they loved me, but I knew they only loved the version of me I let them see. But that was not the real me. I had hidden the real me away from them. But those "I love you"s, the ones that followed me sharing my whole story via text in the middle of their work day, those were the first real ones. Now I knew they truly loved *me*.

III

THESE ARE THE WAYS

45

NOT MY KID

"I need to show you something." Maddox said with a voice so tiny I could barely hear him. We were sitting in his bed, preparing for bedtime. He was now in middle school and I knew a bedtime routine wouldn't last much longer, so I cherished each one. His eyes didn't leave his quilted blanket as he tried to muster the courage to say what he had to say. "Please don't be mad."

I didn't know the true weight of modern parenthood until I was looking at a self-inflicted wound on my child's body.

For the last several years, I had been working as a Researcher/Office Manager at one of the best children's counseling centers in Atlanta. I had somehow stumbled on the most amazing boss who saw potential in me and took me under her wing as a mentor. She saw I had a knack for reading mental health research studies and interpreting them into layman's terms, and she encouraged me to embrace it. For that reason, I knew the statistics for self-harm. I knew it was a rising epidemic in tweens and teens. I knew 1 in 5 young people engaged in it and that number was rapidly rising. I knew I shouldn't blame myself, because the amount of digital and social exposure to self-harm was way too much for any parent to navigate. But once it hit my doorstep, all I could do was feel that I had failed him.

"Sweetie, did you do this to yourself?" I asked.

"Yes." he said, with a hesitancy that can only be explained by shame.

"Why?" I asked, fighting back tears and hoping with all my might I wouldn't scare him back into his shell with my response. I knew if I used the wrong tone he would withdraw.

"My girlfriend does it. I hate how much pain she is in. I wanted to know what it felt like to be her so maybe I could help show her how to fix it."

In 6th grade Maddox met a person that illuminated for all of us that he deeply struggled with anxiety. He had shown signs of being a saver and a people pleaser all his life. I knew this, because I wore it like a badge of honor. I was the nice boy's mom. He was the only person the girl in class with Selective Mutism spoke to. The teachers picked him to walk the sick and injured kids to the nurse's office because they knew he was comforting and they could trust him. Parents asked if their kid could hang out with him because he would be a good influence on them. Until I saw the cut marks, I hadn't seen any of those things as warning signs because I was too busy showing them off.

Then he went through puberty. All of the intense feelings and profound empathy collided and became an incredible burden on his shoulders. When he met this particular person, she was the first person who seemed to also struggle with the weight of the world. He thought she got him, because she was miserable inside too. He was happy to meet all of her needs because, in return, she made him feel a little less crazy. Unfortunately, she had a lot of needs.

We saw changes in his behavior, like pulling away into his room and no longer spending time with us, but we chalked it all up to "he's a tween". Then, I guess the burden became too much to bear one night and it all broke like a flood. That's when he showed me his arm.

"Oh, sweetie. I'm so sorry. Hurting yourself is not going to help her. It never does. She needs help and so do you."

"She said she's going to kill herself, mom. I have to do something to save her. I don't know what I would do if she died. You can't tell anyone because then she might get even more sad and actually do it. She made me swear not to tell anyone. She'll break up with me if I do."

I went to work the next day, never more grateful to work among Atlanta's best mental health professionals. I shared with my boss, Dr. Megan Mann, what happened and asked her to remind me again what the hell I'm supposed to do now.

"It's so awful," she said, "Today's kids live in such a pressure cooker. It's inescapable for any family."

"What do you mean?" I asked, unable to see my own child amongst my research.

"They are all expected to go to college. Not only that, but the *best* college. Parents feel like failures if their child doesn't get into the top 10% of schools. Did you know kids who live in high academic pressure environments have a *higher* risk of anxiety, suicide, and depression than kids who life in impoverished and high-crime areas? We start prepping them for Ivy League out of the womb and it's ruining them. The kids are trying to live up to these impossible standards all while they are being bombarded on the internet with the most harmful content. Do you know how easy it is for a kid to come across a self-harm tutorial online? So easy. Much easier than accessing healthy therapeutic tools. If your kid isn't falling apart, their friend is. Maddox and his girlfriend are a part of a new normal for adolescents, and it's heartbreaking."

Her words stung a little because I could see myself when she described the pressure-cooker parents. I had been part of the problem. Now seeing the impact it had on Maddox, I was asking myself why *had* less than the top 10% become defined as failure? I remembered the high achieving parents I became enamored by at Maddox's preschool. The ones I tried to emulate because I thought they had it all figured out. I was following them right off a cliff and I didn't even realize it. I trusted them to have the answers because they had the money. I was trying to give my kid options, and instead I gave him an anxiety disorder.

Not only was I to blame by bragging on his people pleasing and pressuring him academically, but that wasn't all. I'm also the one who shoved "be kind" down his throat 24/7. I'm the one who constantly talked about the "other guy's" perspective and how we have to think of others' feelings when we make choices. He watched me give myself away to any and everyone in order to earn being worthy of their love. I was so obsessed with raising a nice, gentle man that I didn't realize I already had one, and I was breaking him. I was suffocating him with empathy. He didn't need those lessons. He needed to be told how to set boundaries, how to say no, and how to recognize what *his* needs were… all things I couldn't teach him because I didn't know how to do them myself.

As I started to make a plan for how to help him, I realized my plans of breaking generational cycles were dashed. Everything I did as a parent was with the hopes of keeping him out of therapy as an adult. And now he had barely made it to middle school and already needed a therapist.

I wanted so badly to break the cycle with him. I couldn't love myself, but I could raise someone who could love themselves. I couldn't manage my anxiety, but I could raise someone who knew how to manage theirs. As I was researching therapists for him, it became abundantly clear that if I wanted to break generational cycles, I was doing it backwards. *I* had to break them, starting with *me*. I had learned to let others love me but I still hadn't learned to love myself. Trying to raise someone who was "not me" had caught up with me.

Maddox was like me, a lot like me - and he knew I hated that. I had to learn to accept it. Hell, I had to love it.

46

MEDITATION

Deep breath in... deep breath out.

What is a deep breath exactly? Ten seconds? Right?

Deep breath in...

One... two... three... four... am I guessing right about how long a second is? Maybe I'm counting too short. Maybe I'm counting too long. Oh crap! Five... Six... good god how long have I been holding my breath?!

A burst of air aggressively departed my lungs.

Dammit. Ok, let's try again.

Deep breath in... deep breath out.

Ok, I'm supposed to be clearing my mind. Does thinking about clearing your mind count? Does asking about thinking about clearing your mind count?

Deep breath in...

What does a clear mind look like? Like, are some people's minds actually blank? Or is it, like, blank except for one voice that's saying 'breathe in, breathe out'? I don't think I've ever had a totally blank mind. Is that like a coma? What do people in comas actually feel?

At the same time that the coma rabbit hole began, the alternate voice in my head started doing its own thing.

First meditate, then grocery shop, don't forget to make a list first. Milk, bread, sugar...

And at the same time, the alternate alternate voice started doing its own totally *other* thing, in a sing-song voice for no apparent reason.

Hum dee dum dum... I loooove treeeees... Trees are coooool...

I became aware of the three simultaneous voices and let out a hard sigh.

Oh my god! Shut up, brain!

Aggressive breath out...

I suck at meditating. This is pointless.

I finally gave up, rolled up my mat, and walked away. I had attempted meditation a thousand times throughout my life. Every therapist recommended it and said it would be the key to a clear mind.

I guess I'm just too broken and can't fix this loud ass brain.

I got into my car and put it on *Awake My Soul* by Mumford and Sons. My body relaxed to the music and as I sang along my brain melted into the melody. All of my voices aligned in a concert of joy.

The sky is so pretty today. Life is going to be ok. Awake my soul. I have a beautiful family. I am so grateful for this day.

It took me a while to realize I had been meditating the majority of my life. Hell, I was practically a master at it. I was just reading the wrong rule book for meditation. I had the standard rule book that stated "Meditation must be done in silence with the goal of clearing your mind." The neurodiverse rule book was much more useful. It said, "Our minds are never quiet. So use music or nature to get the many symphonies in my brain in sync. Then they will play healing and loving messages to you." Once I made it intentional, you couldn't stop my meditation game. I'd give myself a song or a hiking trail to focus on, and then let the meditation align in perfect harmony.

47

THE CASE OF THE MISSING GRILL BRUSH

I had an original chore: fold the laundry. In order to fold the laundry, however, I needed to clear the breakfast dishes from the dining table because I did laundry on the dining table. When I cleared the dishes from the table so that I could fold the laundry, I realized the sink was now full of dishes, so the dishes needed to be done. When I went to fill the dishwasher with the dirty dishes, I realized it was full of clean dishes that needed to be put away. While I was putting away the clean dishes, I had trouble fitting all of the clean tupperware into the tupperware drawer. I nearly severed a finger trying to shove the tupperware in and slam the drawer shut. That was when I decided that in order to do the laundry, I must declutter all of the kitchen cabinets and drawers. It's like the book *If You Give a Mouse a Cookie,* except way less exciting and at the end there was no cookie, just a ransacked kitchen.

I was very discerning about what was kept. I learned to love minimalism as a way of managing my messiness. It's hard to make a mess when there is less stuff to make a mess with. So every time I discarded something it felt like success. I pillaged through every drawer, cabinet, and cupboard. No dish would survive without proving its usefulness to me. In the end I had two cardboard boxes and two trash bags full of discarded items. Not only did the tupperware drawer have plenty of space, but now I felt the urge to go out and buy new tupperware because this old spaghetti-stained crap didn't deserve my perfectly organized drawer. I walked away feeling quite satisfied with myself, the laundry pile watched me cross the room from afar, totally untouched.

Later that evening, I heard Brad in the kitchen, "Hey, did you throw away my grill brush?"

"No. I hate that thing so I almost did, but I knew you'd kill me so I didn't." I pondered for a brief moment, "Yeah, I'm positive I didn't."

"Are you sure? I don't see it anywhere," he said as he frantically shuffled in the kitchen drawers. My memory suddenly became less clear and I started to question my confidence. Then I remembered that, while I had debated whether to throw it away or keep it, in the midst of a minimalistic high, I had in fact decided to give it away, Brad's feelings be damned. My body tensed up. *Fuck.*

"Yes. I'm sure I didn't throw it away." I lied. My heart started beating fast. My total focus at this point was on evading capture as the grill brush thief.

"That's weird. I don't see it anywhere… and you just cleaned out the whole kitchen…" he said, likely genuinely confused. But all I heard was the accusation of being a big fat liar, which was the only thing worse than being a grill brush thief.

"I didn't throw away the damn grill brush! Stop blaming me for something I didn't do!" I snapped.

"Ok, ok. I was just saying it seemed strange. It's fine, I'll just buy a new one."

He spoke so casually, as if I was not on the trial of my life here. Every second that passed I was sinking deeper and deeper into guilt. *How is it, after all these years, I am still a liar? How could I lie to the person I love most in the world?* The tension became agony and I decided to do the riskiest thing I've possibly ever done. I decided to confess.

"Ok," I sighed, "I think I threw the grill brush away. I lied to you." At this point I started to cry, despite my pre-plan not to. "I don't know why I lied. I didn't remember at first but then after a while I realized I probably did. I just didn't feel like I could tell you. I think I am scared to be wrong. Like if I'm wrong I lose the right to be loved or respected or something. I just don't feel like I can make any mistakes. This is why I think I might secretly be a bad person. Because what good person lies about something that stupid?! And if I can't even tell the truth about *that*, what other horrible things might I lie about if I didn't keep myself in check?!" I dropped my head in my hands, not feeling that distant from the girl crying on the shitty brown couch. And just like back then, instead of running for the hills, Brad calmly took my hand.

"It's ok, I understand. You are not a bad person because you lied about a grill brush. It's ok."

But it didn't feel ok. It didn't feel like no big deal. It felt huge and endless and terrible and cruel. It felt like I was confessing to the worst crime. I wondered if Brad said it was no big deal because he was scared of me finding out I'm a bad person, or because maybe it actually wasn't a big deal.

"I think I might need to try therapy again," I said. Brad didn't disagree.

I was ready to close the case once and for all: *Am I a good person or a bad person trying really hard to seem like a good person?*

48

RAPID RESOLUTION THERAPY

Finding the right person to help me figure out whether I was a good or bad person was going to be tricky. I had done about all I could do from a therapist's couch. I worried that as long as my conscious brain was in charge I would keep trying to fool my therapists into liking me, thus their assessment of me as a "good person" would be unreliable. I heard about a social worker in my area who did something called Rapid Resolution Therapy. A quick Google search revealed a vague description of something that involved hypnosis. The reviews of this woman swore they got what they needed in one or two three-hour sessions. That definitely sounded like my kinda healing - quick, affordable, and deep in the subconscious.

I was scared of opening up my subconscious, but I knew it was necessary. After a lifetime of fighting it into submission, I was about to crack it open and see what was behind the curtain, for better or worse. Even if I didn't like what I saw, I just needed to know what was there.

I met the RRT lady at a barn that had been converted into an Airbnb. As she mentioned several times, she was temporarily living there since her recent separation from her husband. She wore a flowy, colorful caftan and had a Pomeranian that followed her wherever she went. She looked and sounded almost identical to Jennifer Coolidge (aka "Stiffler's Mom" on *American Pie* or the lady from *The White Lotus*). She cleared away a pile of Bohemian clothing from her chaise lounge so I could lie down.

I looked around the barn/apartment/divorcee sanctuary at all of the crystals, clothing, and clutter that was around me. *Where the hell am I? What the hell am I doing? What is a reason I can give this woman for why I need to get up and leave right now?*

Ultimately, in an effort to not humiliate this woman who was already going through enough, I decided to stay. I would just go through the motions for the next few hours and then cut out of there on two wheels and never look back.

"Why are you here?" Jennifer Coolidge asked.

"To find out if I'm a bad person or not." I replied.

"Well, you're not. I can tell."

I appreciate that, Jennifer. But I've fooled quite a lot of people into liking me, so forgive me if I don't believe you. Plus I don't think years of self-hatred will be solved by the opinion of someone who, I'm pretty sure, needs this more than I do.

"Yeah, but, I think that's the problem," I said, "Everyone *thinks* I'm a good person. I'm worried I'm really good at fooling people into thinking that. I'm just ready to let go and know the truth."

Without any acknowledgement of my response and with zero attempt to segway, Jennifer jumps right into the next segment of her session.

"So let's say there is a tiger in the room. You have four possible fear responses..."

"Yes, I know about fear responses..." I said, hoping she could read between the lines and know, *Hey, I study these responses for a living, so, let's move on.*

"There's fight: with a fight response you would punch the tiger."

"Yes, I know."

"There's flight: with a flight response you run from the tiger."

"Right, and freeze."

"Freeze: with freeze you go numb and do nothing and hope you survive whatever happens."

I nodded my head to be polite but inside my brain was on fire just wanting her to hurry the hell up. I just sat with crossed arms and waited for her to wrap up the speech that she was so clearly hell bent on giving.

"And fawn: with fawn you try to make friends with the tiger and hope that he doesn't hurt you."

"Oh." I paused, "I actually haven't heard of fawn before. That sounds like a response I may have done a lot in my life."

"Yeah. Your brain basically sees everything as a threat and is stuck in that fear response. So you fawn all the time and that makes you feel like a fraud, like you're fooling everyone into liking you. That is why you're afraid you're a bad person, because you are just trying to ensure no one hurts you."

"Oh. Huh." *Whaa? This bitch might not be crazy after all.*

I had been fawning my whole life. I started to question that maybe I wasn't a masochist sicko who loved abuse and chaos. I was fawning to survive. I was fawning with my stepbrother, Jesse, when he molested me. I was fawning with Mama when I wrote that award-winning love letter to Brach's candy. I have been fawning with every asshole coworker, toxic boyfriend, or dominating friend my entire life. My brain just hoped I could be so lovable that they would stop hurting me.

I started to feel a little more comfortable with ole Jenny C. Maybe the answer to my question did in fact lie in a barn-turned-Airbnb that was covered in as much dog hair as it was crystals and smelled intensely like patchouli. Finally, after the cognitive portion of the session, it was hypnosis time.

She started with a guided meditation and some breathing exercises. I knew I wasn't highly hypnosable (I had tried once at a county fair) so I didn't have high expectations for how deep I would go.

"Imagine a timeline of your life," she said in her most Coolidge-esque voice, "Imagine each moment has a sheer curtain hanging between it. Keep walking through curtain after curtain until you come to a curtain that is opaque. When you reach that curtain I want you to take three deep breaths and then lift the curtain and enter that moment in time. Tell me what you see once you are there."

With little to no effort, sheer curtains began to lift in front of me. Me feeling itchy from rolling in the grass with Maddox for too long. Me clogging (tapdance for country people) onstage at the county fair as a child. Me and Brad on a date night, tasting craft beers and talking about our futures. Me at Daddy's wedding to Little Mama, wearing a dark green flower girl's dress. Everyone else wore pink dresses but Daddy let me wear my favorite color because I hated pink. It stuck out like a sore thumb in all the photos but he didn't mind. It was hard to leave that moment but I knew I needed to let the curtain lift. Then came the opaque one. I felt myself trying to guess what was on the other side before I lifted it.

It's probably the moment I found out Daddy was dead? Nope. Please don't be the moment in college when that guy pantsed me when I wasn't wearing underwear because it was laundry day and everyone called me Bush behind my back (which was not very behind my back at all)? Thank god, it's not that either.

I finally just let go and decided to let the moment reveal itself. *Breath one. Breath two. Breath three.* Then the curtain lifted.

"I'm there."

"What do you see? Tell me every detail as it unfolds."

"I see Pal, my sister. We're in my bedroom at the log cabin I grew up in. The one I moved into after she moved out. I must be eight or nine. I know she's 15 so I must be nine. She's visiting. There's no bedroom for her in this house, just my room. We're playing video games. I'm being silly, trying to entertain her. There's nothing significant about this moment I don't think. Why am I seeing this?"

"Stay with the moment. Listen to it. Ask it, 'what is significant about this moment'?"

I listened for an answer. "I'm being over–the-top. Trying to be entertaining. I am trying hard to let Pal know I'm happy and ok. Because..." I gasp. Tears start to well up.

"What is it?"

"I know she isn't coming back."

"Why isn't she coming back?"

"Because she can't take it anymore. She hates it here. She only comes here because of me. I know she's getting tired of seeing Mama and Larry. She hasn't said she's never coming back but I just know this is the last time. I don't know how. I want her to know it's ok for this to be the last time. I'm trying to let her know it's ok by acting so happy. I want her to think that I'm ok here alone."

"Are you ok there alone?"

I took a moment to just let the tears stream down my face. I had never felt cathartic tears like these before. I had cried out of sadness and anger a million times, mostly only in front of Brad. I had cried of joy only once, when Maddox was born. I had never cried cathartically. I was ready to release a truth I had been hiding my whole life.

"I'm not ok. I am heartbroken and devastated but you can't tell from the outside. I spent so much time trying to make people think I was ok and I almost never was. That's what I wanted more than anything. For no one to be able to tell I wasn't ok."

I normally would never allow myself to cry in front of anyone, at the top of that list a woman in a caftan with a Pomeranian. But nothing mattered more to me in that moment than that little girl who held in her tears for so long. I let her have them, Pomeranian be damned.

"Now tell me," said JC, "is that little girl a good person or a bad person?"

I had to smile through my tears at the ridiculousness of the question. "Of course she's not a bad person." I sat for a moment and let that realization, and all the heartache that came with it, sink in. "She is so good. She's not only good, she is the brightest ball of light that I have ever seen."

49

GOOD PEOPLE WITH MESSY ROOMS

"Maddox Rome," Brad said in a deep, serious tone that was always deeper and more serious than he intended. "Clean your room. I have asked you ten times and you still haven't done it."

"But-" Maddox started.

"No. No more excuses. It's ridiculous how messy it is in there. Go."

Maddox headed to his room, shoulders slumped. Brad walked in the living room and collapsed on the sofa next to me. I could feel the heat of frustration radiating off of him. I had purposefully removed myself from the conversation, yet I knew that sofa-plop meant I was about to be very much part of the conversation.

"He is so stubborn sometimes." Brad said with irritation in his voice.

I didn't say anything.

"He just seems so entitled to me." he reinforced, waiting for some validation. He let out one more hard sigh and I knew I had reached the end of my attempt at staying out of it.

"Or…" I started, but then trailed off, hoping my vague suggestion of there being more to the story would be enough for him to see things differently.

"What?" he asked.

"Maybe he's something other than stubborn or entitled."

"What do you mean? I've told him so many times to have his room clean by the end of the weekend, and here it is almost bedtime on Sunday and it's still not done. Earlier, when he *said* he was cleaning his room, I went in to check on him and his floor was an even *bigger* mess because he had pulled a bunch of stuff out of his old toy chest and he was, as he put it, 'being nostalgic.'"

I laughed. Perhaps poorly timed, but I don't get to pick when things are hilarious.

"It's not funny!" he said. "He has to learn to take better care of his things."

"Ugh! 'Take better care of his things.'" I said with mockingly over-the-top mimicked air quotes and a sarcastic tone to match. "I heard that my whole life. Everyone assumed that because I was messy I was lazy, stubborn, entitled and *didn't take care of my things*."

"How is being messy taking care of your things?"

"Is there really a huge difference between a pile of clean clothes in the corner and clean clothes in a drawer?"

"Wrinkles."

"He puts them in the dryer. He looks nice when he leaves the house. He's a nice person. Why do we need more than that?"

"Because it's our job to teach him how to do these things."

"Actually, tidiness is highly genetic." I might as well have put on a pair of nerdy glasses, a lab coat, and pulled up a podium. "It is not likely we will 'teach' him anything. As he grows, he will find where he fits on the tidiness spectrum. And in fact, *making* him act like a different type of tidy person than he really is hinders that process."

"Don't start with the statistics and research again, please..."

"But statistics and research matter. In the end, a parent's influence and guidance only account for about 10% of who a person ultimately becomes. Genetics outweigh that factor by a *lot.* Do you really want to argue with him over something that will have a 10% influence? It's not a wise investment. Just leave it alone."

Brad let out another hard sigh. This is not the first time I prioritized data and research over his need for validation. It's annoying.

"Plus," I said (because I can't let a sleeping dog lie), "you don't know how it feels when people make assumptions about your character based on stupid stuff like how clean your room is."

"Character assumptions? I'm not doing that."

"Yes you are. You're not just saying 'You have a messy room and that makes me uncomfortable'. You're saying 'You're stubborn and entitled'. Like I said before, maybe he's something other than stubborn and entitled..."

Brad looked at me blankly, clearly eluding wasn't enough.

"Maybe he's a good person... with ADHD."

Yup. It turned out Maddox was a neurospicy just like me. He was also gifted, so his assignments would be in disarray and he could still pull off As.

Brad saw my point (and it's hard to argue with a spouse who specializes in working with neurodivergent teens about whether or not your teen is neurodivergent). We stopped making him clean his room. Most of the time it looked like a nuclear bomb went off. Sometimes he hyper focused on cleaning and it would be spotless in an hour. But whether clean or messy, we didn't determine things about his character based on the state of his room. We learned how to parent ADHD without shaming it. Lo and behold, he didn't become an entitled, stubborn, or lazy human. In fact, he blossomed into one of the most phenomenal teens I'd ever met... with a mostly messy room.

50

PANIC AT THE OCEAN

I get a lot of crap for not being a big fan of beaches. To be clear, I don't *hate* beaches, I'm just not a big fan. Especially the kinds of beaches that are lined with resorts. I'm always confused when beach-lovers talk about how "relaxing" or "lowkey" their beach vacation was. Whatever they're experiencing, I haven't experienced.

Every beach resort vacation I've ever been on goes the same way. Overflowed arms filled with beach chairs, umbrellas, "portable" coolers, towels, and buckets of sunscreen as I traverse an endless stretch of flesh-melting, unsteady sand. Only to arrive at a mountain of seaweed and the sensory nightmare that is sweat, sand, and saltwater. And then when I'm ready to leave, which is almost immediately, I have to do that same horrific trek back, only this time with a wet bathing suit and brutally chafed thighs. Sweat is pouring down my face, (because it is *always* hot at the beach) burning my eyes and making it nearly impossible to see. There is no hope of wiping the aforementioned sweat away because both arms are weighed down with a dozen straps to a dozen items, all of which are sawing their way through the flesh of my forearms and shoulders. And speaking of my shoulders, they are almost certainly sunburned despite the near constant application and re-application of sunscreen. When I finally do complete the endless journey back to the hotel room, it is freezing inside, causing a rapid shift from 3rd degree burns to near hypothermia. Now, regardless of what I do to try and stop it, I will inevitably track sand all through the hotel room which will eventually end up in my bed, keeping me up all night. And the next day, for some ungodly reason, everyone wants to go out and do it all again, as that is the only thing to do at the beach. My only reprieve is the one hour hot-ass shower I will take before dinner when, for a brief moment, I do not have sand in every crevice of my body. Repeat that process until the vacation finally comes to a close and I wish to god I had scheduled some additional time off before having to immediately return to work after a week of overstimulation, sunburn, and sheer disappointment.

Every few years I run out of excuses to give beach-loving Brad as to why we should go anywhere but the beach. The summer of 2021 was such a summer where I could delay no longer. We went to New Smyrna Beach in Florida for the quintessential beach experience.

The boys bought boogie boards to capitalize on the towering waves the beach was experiencing that week. I happily stayed back where I, and the toddlers in swim diapers, felt a little more comfortable. In spite of being much more comfortable on my end of the ocean, I had a hard time being left out of their fun. I was reminding myself a little too much of Mama. I had countless memories of her ruining trips because she was too scared of something. Once we made her ride the Free Fall at Six Flags and she cried, made us leave immediately, and yelled at us for the rest of the afternoon. So, in an effort to prove myself un-Mama-like, I headed deeper into the ocean to join them and give boogie boarding a try. The waves were insanely choppy. They were pushing me in two directions at once, testing the laws of physics in their contradiction. It felt like however I tried to prepare for a wave was always the wrong way. The boys watched me, proudly, waving at me to keep going. *Just keep going,* I thought. *Don't be the lame mom.*

They kept saying "the waves get calmer further out" but they were starting to rise over my head and I began to question if both of them being over 6' tall may alter their perception of my safety somewhat. Every time I made it closer to them, a wave came in and knocked me further back.

"I don't think I'm gonna make it that far." I said, and began to turn back.

"Come on, you can do it!" Brad said as he walked to meet me.

"No, I'm too uncomfortable... I don't think I can."

"Come on, I'll lead you. Just follow me." He grabbed my hand and pulled me towards him. A big wave came and slapped me right in the face, knocking me over, igniting a panic attack.

I hadn't had a panic attack in years. My chest tightened and my eyes welled up with tears. I felt a burning heat all over my face. My lungs felt like a snake had entered my body and was coiling itself around them. The waves had no sympathy either, they just kept beating the shit out of me. It felt like they were mocking me. Brad stood beside me, not sure what to do.

"Are you ok?" he asked.

"No! I'm not ok at all!" I said, aggressively wiping away my tears, "I'm having a fucking panic attack!" I turned my back to the shore so all of the people wouldn't see the crazy lady crying in the ocean.

"I was just trying to help you. I thought you wanted to come out further with us."

"No, I don't *want* to go out further. I feel like I *have* to or I get left behind. I told you I wasn't comfortable!"

"I thought that meant you wanted my help. You don't have to get mad at me." A defensiveness brewed in his voice.

"I don't have time to reassure *your* feelings right now. Give me some space," I said, bitingly.

Brad didn't like someone being angry with him, that was always a big trigger. But I didn't have time to think of his triggers, I was too busy trying to manage mine. He walked away and left me alone, defeated.

Meanwhile, my mind was racing. I tried to stay present with it. Normally, I would have responded to a public panic attack by slapping some big ole anger armor on it and lashing out. While I had bitten Brad's head off a teensy bit, it was sugarplums and lollipops compared to the rage I felt inside. I allowed the tears to flow and along with them my feelings.

Why is this such a big deal?! Why am I having a panic attack in the ocean?!

I want to get out of this ocean. I want to go back to the hotel room and pout in private where it's safe. I want to stay there for the rest of the day and make Brad pamper me until I feel better. This is all his fault.

No. That's what Mama used to do. She'd just ruin the whole day. I need to get these feelings out now so I don't ruin the whole vacation trying to suppress them. I'm going to stay here, dammit. And it's not Brad that's the problem, either. It's the ocean, it's triggering something. I'm going to beat this ocean and my trigger. I need to just stay present, feel my feelings.

The ocean violently jerked me side to side, front to back, knocking me off balance at every turn, but I didn't leave. I let the tears fall. The waves were cruel. I kept walking up and down the shoreline, but never allowed myself any shallower. Eventually, normal breathing became more accessible, I was able to check in with my body. This feeling was familiar, and that's why it was so painful.

This is how I felt for so much of my life. Unsteady, never able to get proper footing. Always trying to guess the right next step that would lead to safety and always being wrong. These waves are showing me my internal experience throughout my life. I pondered what Brad pulling me into the deep triggered. *So many times I was uncomfortable and no one seemed to care. All those boys who took advantage of me knew I was uncomfortable, but they didn't care. Uncomfortable should mean "no" or "stop". Why is it when I say no, no one hears me?*

New tears emerged. These weren't panic tears, these were healing tears. I was grieving. Grieving all the times I screamed "No!" from inside my soul but did not know how to make the words loud enough for people to listen to them. Grieving all the times other people decided what was best for me without ever asking me. Grieving all the times someone told me to hold my discomfort in so they wouldn't have to feel it. I sat in the ocean, right out in plain view for everyone to see, and I grieved. I felt such deep empathy for the young girl who carried this feeling throughout my life.

As my mood shifted from anger, to grief, to compassion, I realized something. The main reason I wanted to go in the deep end of the ocean in the first place was to not be like Mama. I thought in order to not be like her I had to be able to go in the deep end of the ocean. But that wasn't it. I am sensitive like her. I do have limitations other people don't seem to have. But that's not what ruined my childhood vacations. It was the fact that she couldn't handle those limitations with compassion and grace. She couldn't allow her family to do brave things without her. She couldn't allow herself to have limitations. I could have a panic attack in the ocean and then choose to move on. She could never move on. She needed someone to blame, someone to validate her. I don't have to need those things.

I made two promises to myself before leaving that ocean:

From now on, when I say "No" people will hear it.

I will let my family go in the deep end of life, even if I can't join them.

51

FATHER FIGURES

"Did you see what Aunt Tami shared on Facebook?" Pal texted me.

"No, what is it?" I asked, as I simultaneously went to Facebook to see what she was talking about.

Before I could find it, she replied "Uncle Don has cancer."

Despite him and Daddy being best friends and brothers, and me having grown up playing with his sons like they were my siblings, I had lost touch with Uncle Don over the last couple of decades.

Uncle Don was the obvious candidate to step in as my surrogate father after Daddy died. But unfortunately, he couldn't bring himself to fill that role. He blamed himself for Daddy's death. He was with him when he died and he thought if he had known CPR he could have saved him. At Daddy's funeral he burst into tears and fell at our feet, crying "I'm so sorry" over and over. Even though we never once blamed him, he could not stop blaming himself. The guilt grew heavy and he inadvertently distanced himself from us. I'm sure he felt like we didn't want him around, and we were hurt that he wasn't around. No one knew how to talk about any of that, so we mutually drifted apart.

When I first heard he had cancer I mailed him a get-well card and sent word through other family members that I was thinking about him. With all of the distance, I didn't think it was my place to do more than that. I felt bad for his situation and knew he was the last person who deserved it, but I never considered the toll losing him would take on me, because I had barely spoken to him in almost 20 years.

Then he entered hospice and suddenly everything changed. Shit got real and it was time to say goodbye. Pal and I went to the hospital and it was instantly as if no time had passed. I regretted the distance and thought of all the wasted years that had gone by. Unfortunately, by the time I had that realization he was so heavily sedated that he was incoherent and unable to speak. I held his atrophied hand and told him I loved and missed him. I told him I was sorry for not seeing him sooner. I told him it was ok to let go, because Daddy was waiting for him on the other side. All the while, his current wife was whispering in his ear for him not to leave. I felt resentful towards her, but then realized I know nothing about their relationship. I had missed so many years of his life, his wife and even his children felt like strangers. The next day he passed away, on the exact same day as his big brother and best friend, 26 years to the day, on November 29th. Needless to say, November 29th is not my favorite day.

At his funeral, I saw someone I hadn't seen in just as many years. Someone I didn't expect to be there because I didn't know he was still close with my Uncle Don. But, in fact, they had not only remained close, he was one of the pallbearers. My Uncle Thomas.

Uncle Thomas was married to Daddy's sister, Aunt Tami, back when Daddy died. My uncle-in-law, I guess would be the proper term. He was the unexpected contender for my new father figure that I never saw coming. Before Daddy died, I wasn't particularly close with him. He played golf with Daddy, I saw him at family functions, and he was a nice enough guy, but with two other "real" uncles I never paid him much attention. But after Daddy died, he showed up more than anyone else and in ways I couldn't have imagined. When I was such a problem for everyone else, he never seemed burdened by me. I felt so unconditionally loved by him. He had his own children and stepchildren to raise but always seemed to have time for me. He taught me how to play softball and, when I freaked out at softball sleepaway camp, he came to pick me up even though Little Mama told him not to because she thought I was just doing it for attention. Maybe he knew I needed the attention. Daddy left big shoes to fill, massive actually, but for Thomas those shoes seemed to fit perfectly.

We remained very close until one day, while I was away attempting college for the first time, I got a call from Aunt Tami. She told me she and Thomas were getting a divorce. She just wasn't in love with him anymore. I was devastated and pissed at her. I waited for Thomas to reach out to me so I could take his side and tell him how fucked up it all was, but he never did. And I never called either. We faded out.

It's funny how I could lose touch with two people I loved with all my heart. All because we couldn't have hard conversations.

Seeing Uncle Thomas at Uncle Don's funeral was surreal. I often wondered where he had been all those years. The last place I expected to see him was at a Garrett funeral. He looked exactly the same. Tall, lanky, with a Sam Elliot mustache and a head full of grayish-white hair - which hadn't changed because he had grayish-white hair since I'd known him. After the funeral ended all I could think about was finding him and talking to him.

"Have you seen Thomas?" I asked my Aunt Tami.

"I think I saw him leaving," she replied.

My heart sank. I had so many questions.

"Oh!" she said, pointing to the parking lot, "There he is getting into his truck, over there!"

I took off after him, walking as quickly as a person at a funeral could without looking disrespectful. It just seemed wrong to run at a funeral.

My mind was racing as fast as my feet.

What am I going to say to him when I get to him? 'Hello. How've you been? What the hell happened to you? Also, how did you and Uncle Don stay in touch but not you and me?' Why was he leaving so quickly? Did he leave because of me? Did he not miss me? Did he forget about me? Were those years together maybe not as special to him as they were to me?

I didn't care, I was still going after him. If those years weren't significant to him, that was ok. Understandable even. I was sure he had "adopted" lots of kids, being the kind of guy he was. His real kids probably had friends that had absent fathers or maybe he had a new wife and she had kids he had to help raise. I was probably just one of many people he was a father figure to. I finally made it to the truck, a bit out of breath, and flagged him down. He stepped out, rested his arm on the door frame, and looked at me.

"Well, hey there. How are you?" he said in his perfect Southern drawl.

"Hey! I'm good! How are you?" I said, mirroring his drawl. My natural-born Southern accent was incredibly thick, but I had conditioned myself out of it during the years I was trying to prove myself as a cultured woman, so now it felt phony when I used it. But it didn't feel phony when I used it with Thomas.

"I'm good. Gosh, you're all grown up."

"Yeah, it's been a while. It is so good to see you. I have really missed you a lot. You were so important in my life and when I saw you were here… I just had to see you."

Tears began to well up in his eyes, and mine welcomed them. *He does remember me. I did matter to him too.*

"I have thought about you a million times," he said, "I just didn't… I didn't know how to… just with the divorce and all… it was just too painful. I'm so sorry."

I walked up to him and initiated a hug that, within seconds it was clear, was mutually needed.

"I know. I'm not mad at you at all. *At all.* Do you understand? What you did for me was amazing. I only think fondly of you-"

"No," he interrupted me, "I failed you. I failed your dad."

"What are you talking about?"

"Bill changed my life. Before I met him I was running around wild. I was a deadbeat dad. He straightened me out and showed me how to be a real father. I looked up to that man so much. And I promised him I would take care of ya'll and I didn't. I'm so sorry."

I never knew that about Daddy. I never knew Thomas as anyone other than the most amazing father I had ever met. I had no idea he learned that from my Daddy.

I could see the shame in his eyes and how it had contributed to the silence between us all these years. I wasn't insignificant to him at all, I was *too* significant. I was haunting him every day as a failure in his life. All I could do was hug tighter and hope that was enough to set him free.

"You didn't do anything wrong. I love you and I only think of you as someone who was amazing to me."

He wiped his tears and relieved himself of a small piece of the shame he had been holding onto. He stepped back and looked at me, a gleam in his eye.

"You look so beautiful. Just like you always have."

We exchanged numbers and began texting all the time. I had someone to wish a Happy Father's Day to again. I told him stupid things I was up to and he acted like it was the best thing he'd ever heard. We lived several hours apart now but were planning to meet in the middle for dinner. He said over and over how good it was to have me in his life again. And for me, a hole was filled in my heart that had been empty for a long time.

Just a couple of weeks before our planned meetup he died suddenly of an aneurysm. Just like Uncle Don, I had lived without this man for 20 years, but for him to die just as we were getting back in touch felt immense. More immense than I had patience for. I expected to bounce back quickly. I couldn't make sense of why I was crying all the time and grieving so heavily over someone I had lived just fine without for decades.

As I prepared to go to his funeral, I thought of how I wouldn't know anyone (or at best I would be a vague person in their distant memory). I worried about how intensely I would cry, and how strange that would look to everyone who had no idea who I was. On the way there, I put my "sad" playlist on to try and get the tears out privately ahead of time. About a half hour into my two and a half hour drive, I passed the exit to a nature trail I had gone to several times for healing, and something told me to pull over. My body said, *Don't go to the funeral, go to nature.*

I got out, in my hike-unfriendly funeral clothes and ballet flats and started walking. I had no idea what I was searching for or expected to happen. Shortly into the hike, the tears started falling.

Why all the tears? What is all of this about? Why am I mourning this man that I lived without for so long? How is it I feel like a goddamn orphan? All over again. Again. Two father figures dead within a year. On top of the dead dad that I still haven't gotten over. How can I be expected to keep going when love is always being ripped away? I'm just going to be loving and losing love for the rest of my life. It's never going to end.

I sat down on a tree stump in my depressing black dress, the same one Thomas told me I looked beautiful in a few months before. I looked at the stream that was flowing past. I rested my chin on my hand and felt sorry for myself over something no human is immune to dealing with.

It wasn't long before the sound of the stream called back to the many times I had sought comfort in streams in years past. The sound of the water quieted my anxious thoughts and allowed space for more intuitive thoughts to come forward. I noticed how the stream wove its way through the woods, at its own pace, and how all of the different living things rose out of its bank. Roots of trees reached downward to their water source. A dragonfly landed atop the water for a much needed refreshment. It all flowed so naturally, so sustainably. That's when it hit me.

This is how love is supposed to work. Like how water works in nature. All of these things tap into the water source and take what they need for themselves first. They assume water is abundant. I have to assume love is abundant. And it is abundant when it originates from within. Love is supposed to originate from within just as water nourishes from within. The only love that is guaranteed to be with me until I die is mine. I must love myself first and then send that love outward. I can accept and be nourished by love from others, of course, but my main love source must be me. That is the only sustainable way to be loved and lose love over and over again. I am the only person I know will love me until the day I die.

There Mother Nature was, that annoyingly persistent and sassy little minx, reminding me once again of how important it was to love myself.

52

I'VE GOT A KNIFE

I decided to do a 3-day solo hike on the Appalachian Trail to commemorate all the hard work I had been doing on myself. Being alone with my thoughts was a thing I steadfastly avoided in the past. When Brad and Maddox would go on hunting trips, I would fill every ounce of my potential alone time with friend dates and Netflix binges. I was largely afraid of quiet time and what my thoughts might have to say if I listened to them. Once I knew I was a good person, alone time didn't seem so daunting. In fact, I enjoyed it.

Being alone with myself was one thing, but being alone with myself in the Appalachian Mountains away from civilization was a whole other level. As I did with most things, when the time came to actually do the thing I came up with, I began to wonder why in the hell I felt it was so necessary. As I walked away from my parked car, I never understood more in my entire life what Brad meant when he called me "extra". The first mile didn't help either, as it was extra uphill. I wasn't sure whether the shortness of breath was due to gravity or an oncoming anxiety attack.

Sometime after the first mile, the morning sun had risen just enough so that sunbeams came through the trees. They reflected off little flecks of formica on the ground, creating a glitter effect all around me, as if to say *Welcome Home*. I knew I had made the right decision. I had returned my Inside World back to its rightful place and my inner child was gleaming with delight.

On the first night, I set my tent up off the beaten path. There were campsites all along the Appalachian Trail but I really wanted to give total isolation a try. I hiked about a half-mile onto a side trail and pitched my tent right next to a cascading waterfall. The flowing water gave me life. I set up a little hammock seat facing the waterfall. I used my portable stove to make some ramen noodles with tuna and mayonnaise and ate them by the river bank. After dinner, I made myself a cup of chamomile tea. I even sang a little song out loud. I couldn't remember the last time I sang out loud somewhere other than at home. The solitude was replenishing.

The next day I hiked five miles further to my next campsite, which was at a more populated spot. That campsite was for Brad. He insisted that I be amongst civilization at this stop, just in case my night of solitude was scary rather than sacred. Boy was he wrong. I loved being alone. After having spent the last couple of decades terrified of my brain and thoughts, I had a lot of catching up to do. One night didn't feel like nearly enough. But I didn't want to break my promise to Brad, so I begrudgingly set up camp amongst the humans.

When I arrived at the campsite, there was only one other camper there. He was a barefoot dude with a daypack, assembling an old metal frame tent. He had to have brought it in from nearby, nobody could carry that thing far. I could hear him muttering to himself a lot as I approached. I was headed to get water, and once he saw me he lit up.

"Hey there!" he said.

"Hi." I said, in a friendly-enough way, continuing walking towards the water.

"It's going to be a beautiful night!"

"Yeah it is."

"Are you here alone or do you have people joining you later?"

This is not a question a female hiker ever wants to be asked. Thrown off by the question, I shrugged my shoulders and mumbled an awkward "I dunno..." followed by a quick "Ok! Have a good day!" and power walked the rest of the way to the water source.

As I was gathering water in my canteen, I began to beat up on myself. *Why did I just say 'I dunno'? Why am I scared to lie to this guy and just say people are joining me later? Or better yet, why am I too big of a wuss to tell him that was a rude question. That's probably why I've been such a target to predators my whole life.* Then, upon returning with my water, I noticed he had moved campsites and was now set up right next to mine.

Ok, that's pretty creepy. I thought.

He tried to make more conversation as I arrived back to my site, but I pretended like I didn't hear him and went straight into my tent. I sat down on my sleeping bag and my chest started pounding. The fear center of my brain was clearly sensing a threat.

I had spent the last few years trying to train my brain to ignore my threat sensors. My brain had grown to be overactive and saw threats everywhere. A sarcastic eyeroll from a friend felt like I was in danger of losing that friend. A restaurant I hadn't been to before threatened to not have anything for me to eat. A small criticism from Brad felt like my marriage was in peril. It had become hard to distinguish the real threats from the fake. But this time I agreed with my brain that this cause for alarm was real.

I am miles from any road. I have no idea when we will see another hiker. He moved his campsite next to mine, which there was no logical reason for him to do. He gives me the creeps. It is not unreasonable to think this man really might rape or kill me.

I had always wondered what was worse. To be raped or be killed. When I watched true crime I always wondered who had it worse, the murdered victims or the ones left alive to pick up the pieces. I concluded a long time ago that it was irrelevant, because to be raped *was* to be killed for me. I never believed I could survive another rape. If it happened again, I would kill myself.

I engineered my life with that fact in mind. I stopped flirting, so no one would be attracted to me. I never drank more than one drink, so no one could take advantage of me. I watched my drink like a hawk so no one would drug it. I avoided parking garages and walking at night. I did everything I could to avoid it happening again but still had this looming feeling that it was inevitable, I was just counting down the days. I was just trying to live as long as I could until then.

Now here we were. This was going to be the moment it finally happened. I started to cry, thinking of how I had just reached this place of inner peace and how short lived it had been. I didn't want to just roll over and let it happen like every time in the past but I also had no idea what it looked like to do anything else. I took a breath. It's amazing what learning to take a breath could do.

Ok. Here's the deal. That guy might rape me. It's a real possibility. I'm not ready to throw all of this away so soon. Is there any way I can survive if it happens again?

I took a pause and waited for a response from my Intuition. Just like always, she spoke softly. I never used to hear her over my fear.

If this guy rapes me, he rapes me. It was not the rape that destroyed me before. It was the shame. It was not having a safe place to fall after. If he rapes me what will I do this time? I will go straight home and tell Brad, hell, the whole world what happened. I will call the cops and I won't be ashamed. I will not blame myself for being a woman alone in the woods. I'm entitled to these woods. I have every right to be here. I'm here to heal, I'm where I need to be. If he rapes me, he is the only one to blame. That is the difference. He does not hold the power to destroy my soul. I do. I will survive this and if I don't, I died while living.

I grabbed my knife and my mace and I waited. I recorded a video to Brad and Maddox letting them know I was at peace no matter what happened (you know, just in case this mother fucker really did kill me). I barely slept the whole night. But not because of fear. Because of adrenaline racing through my body, ready to protect me at any cost.

As creepy as that dude was, he never touched me. Maybe he was just a guy who seriously lacked social awareness, or maybe the other hikers who showed up later in the day foiled his plans to rape/murder me. Regardless, I'm grateful for him. Thanks to him, I left those woods feeling like a badass who conquered the fear of her own death.

53

A SPIRAL NOT A LINE

Mother's Day of 2022 was approaching and I was excited. I had survived being a mom for 14 years without totally destroying Maddox's life and that was worth celebrating. I never made set plans for Mother's Day. Some years were spent hiking outdoors, some years were brunch and mimosas, and some years I wanted to stay home and cuddle with my family all day in my PJs. One thing that was consistent was that I was in control and I loved that.

In the midst of scheming up that year's plans, I received this text from Mama:

"I have an idea. Ya'll and your families can all come down here and visit me on Mother's Day. We can go swimming in the pool and have fun together. I am the original mother, after all."

Since becoming a mom myself, I had managed to dodge spending actual Mother's Day with Mama (or Little Mama). Pal and I would take Mama out the weekend or the day before, but never on the actual day. I would send Little Mama a nice card with a phone call, or maybe meet up for a mid-week brunch. I was fiercely protective of "my" day.

So I responded to her text, saying "I'm sorry, I already have plans. But we can get together the weekend before or after. Let me know which works best for you!"

To which she replied, "I am sorry I want to spend Mother's Day with my daughters. I thought ya'll could take one day out of your busy schedules but I guess not. That's fine, we will do something some other time. I thought ya'll would want to comfort me after my recent health scare but I guess not."

The recent health scare she was referring to was a biopsy on her cervix that had come back as precancerous cells, but not cancer. There was no further treatment required and as far as we knew she was fine. My initial trauma response was to back down and give her what she wanted in order to regulate her mood and keep the peace. But I'd come a long way, baby, and she wasn't talking to that little girl who couldn't be happy unless she was anymore. I was a Boundaries Ninja. I gathered all my coping tools and quickly laid down the safe boundary I needed. I even sent her a private text so as not to confront her in front of Pal.

"I am sorry you're disappointed that I already had Mother's Day plans. As for your health scare, I am sorry that happened and I do care. But I don't think the only way to show that I care is by seeing you on actual Mother's Day. I have offered the weekend before and after and I will be happy to celebrate you and your health then. You have mentioned before that we have not done much in response to this health scare. If you recall, when I was diagnosed with melanoma, twice," (Yeah, I had melanoma twice but it was always in the baby stages and not that amazing of a story so it didn't make its own chapter.) "I didn't require any help for my recovery then. I am happy with how our relationship balance currently works and I'm sorry if you are not."

Look at those boundaries, I thought, feeling so impressed with myself. *I've really got this whole mental health thing down.*

Mama's response: "I believe I did come over and bring you food, clean your house, and do the dishes when you had your melanoma removed." (I absolutely did not recall that, by the way. Mama's memory always tended to be slightly different than mine.) "It's fine. I am just feeling sorry for myself because I thought ya'll would want to spend time with me. Don't worry, I won't bother you about it again."

I let the texting end at that, rather than continuing a pointless and desperate exchange that would only result in more hurt feelings. *That's ok*, I thought, *she doesn't have to remember things the way I do in order for my memories to be valid. And she doesn't have to feel the same way I do in order for my feelings to be valid.*

Mother's Day came and went, as did the weekends before and after without a word from her. She was still pouting, I assumed, and communicating her disappointment via the silent treatment. Then, about a month later, we received this text:

"Please check your emails."

My stomach tensed up. That was where I always held my anxiety. I guess that explains the IBS. *Here we go*, I thought. *She didn't get her way and now she's written us a letter to tell us what horrible people we are.*

It was common to get concerned follow-up emails from her. Once after a lovely day of shopping, Mama emailed me to say she thought Brad was cheating on me. And another time after I sent her a video of Maddox doing a snow angel challenge in his bathing suit, she sent an email saying he looked unhappy and she thought he didn't feel safe with us.

For many years of my life, her concerned emails directly impacted me. As ridiculous as the content was, I could never just dismiss them. It would throw me off for days or weeks trying to prove to her and myself that everything was ok. Those old feelings didn't die easily. Before opening her email, I used all my coping tools to prepare myself to hear harsh criticisms. I reminded myself of my boundary of not taking whatever she had to say to heart. I took a few deep breaths and felt confident that whatever was in that email I could handle like the

Boundaries Ninja I was.

To My Two Beautiful Girls,

I'm sending this as an email so you can have time to digest the content before we talk and also so you can decide what to tell the kids.

As you both know, I have been on a medical roller coaster for the past nine months trying to find the answer to why I have been having internal bleeding. Last Wednesday when coming out of anesthesia from my biopsy, the doctor said these words: "I could not operate. You have cervical cancer." That sent me on a total freefall and I have been crying and denying ever since.

I'm expecting the worst, but hoping for the best. I know God is watching over me. I really don't feel like talking right now but I will at some point and I'll let you know when. I don't need ya'll to cry with me now, but I will need you to laugh with me when this is all over.

You are my two greatest accomplishments in my 70 years on this earth.

I Love You Both Forever,
Mama

And, with that, the Universe said fuck your boundaries, fuck your coping tools, and fuck you.

54

WELP

Just because she might be dying doesn't mean anything needs to change. I kept repeating that to myself over and over.

She wasn't asking me to do anything, anyway. Since Mama announced her cancer diagnosis, there were only two things she asked of us: play WORDLE together every day and send her pictures of us living our happy lives.

That threw me off. So much so, I even contemplated the possibility that Tommy (the guy she married after divorcing Larry, though they were indistinguishable from one another) had finally snapped and murdered her and he was texting us pretending to be her, Gabby Petito-style. I admit, falling asleep to true crime for my entire adult life may have contributed to that theory.

I was finally able to resolve that fear one day while I was on vacation in Italy. I sent her a picture of me jumping off of a boat we rented in the majestic Lake Garda, Italy, and into the crystal clear lake water. It was an exhilarating moment and I felt grateful to have a photo that captured the joy I was experiencing. I sent the picture to Mama, to keep my promise of sending her proof of us living our happy lives. She responded with, "Don't they have bathing suits in Italy?! It looks like you're wearing skimpy underwear!" (I was wearing a *long sleeve* rash guard with a standard swimsuit bottom). I knew then that her husband hadn't killed her. That was a text only Mama could send.

I kept waiting for her to ask more of me. To ask me to violate my boundaries or guilt trip me for not being there for her more. But it never happened. She rarely gave us details about her cancer or procedures. She dodged the question of what stage her cancer was in. Pal and I debated whether she kept it secret because it was so mild or because it was so advanced. She wouldn't allow us to visit. In fact, she threatened to call the police on us one time when we tried to insist on bringing her flowers in person.

I kept having two recurring nightmares. One where I visited her and she was faking the whole thing. Another where she was so much sicker than she led us to believe. My nightmares reflected my anxieties when I was awake. The news had come conveniently close to when we declined her Mother's Day idea. I wondered if it was all made up to get back at us for being horrible daughters. There were days I felt ashamed for thinking that way and hated that it was so hard for me to support my own (possibly) dying mother who was barely asking for anything. Most days I wondered how much pain she was in and what she must look like after chemo. I wondered if her hair was falling out. I knew it would not be easy for her to lose her hair, she always took so much pride in how she looked.

All I could think or talk about was Mama's cancer. I thought of other people I knew whose parents had cancer. They were consumed with going to doctor's appointments and waiting on the latest lab results. She was asking none of that from me. It was driving me insane. I wanted to be angry at her, but for what? Being too easy to support while she had cancer?

The worse the cancer got the less she seemed to ask of us. One day, on the only phone call we had gotten since the diagnosis months earlier, she had Tommy tell us the cancer had spread and it was now Stage 4. That was the first time anyone mentioned a stage, and it was the worst one. He said the chemo and radiation failed and now all she could try was immunotherapy to prolong her life as much as possible. And still, all she wanted from us was to keep playing WORDLE and living our happy lives.

For our entire childhood, sickness was a way of getting attention and control, and now she had the golden ticket of sicknesses and she wasn't asking for a damn thing.

While she wasn't asking for anything, I knew in my heart I would give everything. My coping tools were a joke. I was stuck in a constant mind spiral. I would stand in the doorway of Brad's home office and just ramble and speculate about what was going to happen. I wondered if her death would set me free. I wondered why I was so selfish to be thinking about my freedom when my own mother was dying. I wondered why I was so angry at her all those years. I wondered why she wasn't asking for more.

Every thought led to Mama's cancer and every conversation had to be about her or I wasn't present for it. I tried talking to Pal about it but she seemed to be able to keep all of her tools intact throughout the whole process. I felt utterly and completely alone in my experience.

It was time for therapy again. I had blamed this woman for most of my childhood trauma, and now she was dying from cancer. That was going to require some serious shit. I was gonna have to take both hands off the wheel. Back to the subconscious we go, only this time even deeper.

As it just so happened, for the previous three years, I had been researching psilocybin-assisted therapy (therapy with the use of psychedelic mushrooms). I knew from clinical trial studies that people with PTSD had an 83% response rate (some improvement in their symptoms) and 75% had a remission rate (significant improvement or no longer qualifying for the diagnosis at all). I had been admiring psychedelic therapy from afar, thinking one day I might try it in the very distant future, after I was a little more healed. It turned out it was going to happen a lot sooner than I expected, when I was a lot more fucked up.

55

JEFF THE SHAMAN

"You have to see my shaman, Jeff."

I was on the hunt for psychedelic-assisted healing. My search began in the most logical, and legal, place: clinical research trials. As a fan of clinical research studies for many years, I would have been psyched to be a part of one. Unfortunately, I didn't qualify for any of them. Some required me to be a military vet and I was pretty sure my stint in basic training, where the majority of my time was spent in a mental hospital, didn't count. Most of them required me to have taken psychedelics before. Despite the fact that I had been accused of being on drugs multiple times, I still had not actually tried any. Don't do drugs, kids, unless one day you want to qualify for clinical trials.

The next legal option I had was ketamine therapy. But when I learned how different ketamine was from psychedelic mushrooms I decided it wasn't for me. Ketamine is an anesthetic to the brain, whereas psychedelic mushrooms increase neural connectivity in the brain. I know both have stacks of science showing they are effective, but for me I wanted to connect rather than numb, even if the difference was only metaphorical.

With my two legal options off the table, it was time to start exploring the safest illegal way to access psychedelic mushrooms. That is when I came across Jeff the shaman. Everyone recommended him. Apparently, you could see Jeff in a group ceremony or individually. He would give you the medicine and perform energy work as you tripped. For some reason, despite all his praises, everything about him made my Intuition squirm.

Jeff was a shaman to the stars. He was a white dude. That was my first red flag. As I researched his background, I discovered he was a tech bro in his previous life before shamanism. Another red flag. He claimed to have "left all of that behind" when he miraculously healed himself (side-eye). Jeff made bank as a shaman. Group sessions were $1,500 each, individual sessions were $2,500, and you could train to be a shaman just like him for a mere $25,000. Maybe it's just me, but if you're a shaman and you're rich, you're probably not doing it right.

Jeff wore a *lot* of linen, especially shirts that were unbuttoned uncomfortably low. He loved wearing gold medallions that represented all of the indigenous cultures he appropriated. Through a little investigating, I learned that Jeff liked telling people how to interpret their psilocybin experiences. And with every interpretation there was always one last lingering question to explore deeper at the next ceremony.

Now, I don't know why Jeff so clearly creeped me out while everyone else worshiped him. It was likely either the abundant amount of childhood trauma that had gifted me with a healthy level of skepticism, or the fact that I've consumed every cult documentary this planet has to offer. Either way, the idea of taking mushrooms and laying my subconscious at the feet of Jeff the shaman was a big *hell no* for me.

It turned out my instincts were likely right. He was later slapped with several lawsuits accusing him of sexual assault and fraud. Fuck you, Jeff. I hope you burn.

So, no clinical trials, no legal options, and *definitely* no shamans. It looked like I was gonna have to do this shit myself. So that's what I did.

I created my own healing path. I unleashed my hyperfixation trait and let it do its thing. I poured over all the published clinical trial research papers I could get my hands on. I looked at how psilocybin had been utilized in various indigenous cultures for centuries (careful not to appropriate more than I had to by focusing on magic mushroom use in Celtic and Nordic traditions, which was the last time *my* blood was indigenous). I researched cults, the CIA, and MK Ultra and learned how mushrooms had been misused so I could avoid any unnecessary mistakes. And last, I listened to my own Intuition. I created my own method of psilocybin-assisted healing that felt right for me. I found a therapist that was willing to work with me to integrate whatever came up after my self-led trips.

My final obstacle was finding out where I would get shrooms from. As someone who never did a drug in her life, but grew up around a lot of drug dealers, the idea of buying mushrooms from *anyone* didn't seem plausible. I just couldn't do it. This was such a sacred and self-empowering process, I wasn't going to hand the most important detail of that process over to a drug dealer.

So I taught myself how to grow them my damn self. The girl with a fear of drugs her entire life and an OCD-level need to follow rules, was about to grow shrooms.

56

THEY REALLY DO LOOK LIKE LITTLE PENISES

I taught myself how to grow my own magic mushrooms. Obviously, I did all of that in my vacation home in Costa Rica, where such a thing would be totally legal and therefore I would get in zero trouble if I shared how I did it. If you have no interest in how I grew my magic mushrooms, feel free to skip this chapter. For everyone else, listen carefully.

Before I share my Costa Rica method, I think I should share a website where you can order the spores (aka mushroom seeds) for psychedelic mushrooms. Again, of course, growing psychedelic mushrooms is not currently legal in the US (and most other developed countries) but viewing the spores under a microscope for taxonomy purposes is. So if someone were a big fungi fanatic, they could order their own spores - you know, only for the purposes or viewing under a microscope - at this website: www.thesporedepot.com

Meanwhile, back in Costa Rica, with my 12 mL syringe of mushroom spores in hand, I was ready to start growing. I chose the mushroom strain called Golden Teacher because it is widely known as the "beginner" shroom (it's easier to grow and its potency is more consistent).

To begin the first phase of growing, I gathered my supplies of: six 6 oz. mason jars, 3 cups of vermiculite, 1.5 cups of brown rice flour, 1.5 cups of water, 3 teaspoons of instant coffee, 3 teaspoons of gypsum, heavy duty tin foil, temperature changing tape (it will change color when it has reached a sanitizing temperature), an 18x18" opaque plastic bin, and a pressure cooker (InstaPot).

To mix the soil for my mushrooms, I combined the instant coffee and the water first. Then I added the vermiculite to the liquid mixture and let it soak for about 5 minutes. Then I added the rice flour and mixed it well. At the end I sprinkled the gypsum and lightly tossed it in. I then added the soil mixture into the 6 oz mason jars and stopped at the bottom of the lip of the jars. I sprinkled a little vermiculite on top, filling the rest of the jar. I then put a piece of til foil on top, large enough to cover the lid and lip of the jars. I then taped around the bottom of the lip of the jar, and then added two pieces of tape over the top of the jar, creating an X shape if you are looking straight down at the top of the jar.

After I did this with all of the jars, I put them into my InstaPot (on top of the egg rack) with about a cup of water and pressure cooked them on high for 20 minutes. Once they were done in the pressure cooker, I kept the lid sealed and let the jars cool completely down overnight while inside. In the meantime, I sanitized my opaque plastic bin and an area in my bathroom with a 10% bleach solution. Contamination was my biggest concern with growing mushrooms, it is very easy for them to be contaminated with mold or bacteria.

The next morning, I moved the jars quickly into the sanitized bin and sealed the lid. I carried the bin to my sanitized bathroom area. Wearing gloves and a mask, I took my syringe of spores (they come in a syringe) and injected 2 mL into each jar (.5 mL into each edge where the tape meets the lip of the jar). I was careful to inject as closely to the edge of the jar as possible, this helps the root system grow better. I then put the jars back into the sanitized bin, sealed it, and left them alone for anywhere from 5-10 weeks while the "cakes" grow (the mycelium - or mushroom root system - will grow to fill the entire jar up until it is one big, white lump aka cake). After one week of mycelium growth I could see it was working, the roots look fluffy and white. If they looked like anything else I would likely have had a problem and would need to take to Reddit feeds or *The Magic Mushroom Bible* (available on Amazon) to try and guess what went wrong.

While I was waiting for the cakes to grow, I built my own terrarium to put them in for phase 2. I purchased a clear plastic bin (around 18x18") and drilled holes every two inches on every side (including the top and bottom). I had to be very careful drilling the holes because the plastic will crack easily, it was definitely an outdoor project because little bits of plastic were everywhere! I then filled the bottom of the bin with about 2 inches of *rinsed* perlite (I just poked holes in the bag and ran it under my sink to rinse it). Then I cut out six small squares of tin foil for me to place the cakes onto.

Once the entire jar was nothing but white mycelium, it was time for phase 2! I removed the tin foil lid, wiped away the vermiculite that was on top, and popped the cakes out in my (gloved) hands. I then placed the cakes in a bowl of water and put them in the refrigerator to soak overnight. The next morning, I rinsed the cakes off well, rolled them in a layer of vermiculite, and placed them on the tin foil inside my terrarium. I sat my terrarium on top of two books to create a little airflow underneath and placed it under a shady window, similar to how you would place a low light plant.

At least three times a day, I misted water around the terrarium and then fanned my cakes off with a handheld fan. I wanted to keep moisture on the sides of the terrarium, but if the water was dripping down I knew it was too wet. Somewhere between a few days and a week later I started to see my first baby shrooms pop up. Every day they doubled in size and new ones were coming up as well.

I harvested the mushrooms when their tops were spreading but the veil underneath hadn't quite broken, I had been told this was the perfect time to harvest. It took me a while to get the hang of it because the veil breaks so quickly, but pretty soon I was able to tell pretty easily when to harvest.

Once my cakes finished producing new mushrooms, I did a 2nd and 3rd "flush" which means repeating the process of rinsing them, soaking overnight, and placing them back in the terrarium (I don't add the vermiculite for the 2nd and 3rd flushes). From the six cakes (doing three flushes) I was able to get around 30 grams of dried mushrooms (fresh mushrooms are about 90% water so that would equal around 300 grams of fresh mushrooms). Considering I only needed between 2-3 grams per therapeutic trip, this was more than enough for my process (roughly 10-15 psychedelic trips).

To dry the mushrooms I placed them on a sushi mat in a clean, dry area when I picked them. For about a week I would turn them daily so they could fully dry out. Then, because there may still be some moisture, I put them in a jar with a silica gel packet and that tends to keep any remaining possible moisture at bay. I knew when they were fully dried out when they snapped when I bent them. I then stored them in a mason jar in a cabinet until I needed them.

When it was time to actually take them, I started with 2.5 grams (because that is what is used in the most successful clinical research trials) and then adjusted to less or more after I saw how that affected me. They taste like eating sticks, which I did not find very appetizing, so I created my own little recipe for taking them. I brought 1 cup of chicken broth, 1 pinch of salt, and 1 dash of curry powder to a simmer. Then I let it cool down to at least 180 degrees (or take off the stove for 2 minutes). Then I poured the broth in a teacup and put the mushrooms in to let them steep for about 1 minute. Then I ate the mushrooms with a spoon and drank the rest of the broth down. This method seems to cause a faster onset of symptoms compared to eating them raw. I was launched off into the other realm within 10 minutes.

57

THE FIRST TRIP

"How are you feeling about your upcoming psilocybin journey?" my therapist asked.

"Freaked out." I answered, honestly.

"That's understandable. The unknown can be scary. Have you been able to set an intention yet?"

It had been my homework since session #1 with my therapist to work on setting my intention. An intention is what you want the focus of the trip to be about, something you want to release or something you want to dive deeper into. But all I could think about was the fear. *What does it feel like to be high on shrooms? What if I have a bad trip? What am I going to act like or say? Will I say anything embarrassing or share a deep, dark secret? Do I really want to open Pandora's box? How can I be sure this won't break my brain or ruin my life?*

"I feel like I'm standing on a cliff blindfolded and being asked to step off of it, and I have no idea how high it is. It's hard to focus on an intention when I have no idea what it will do to me."

"I wish I could give you peace of mind about what your experience will be like, but I can't," she said, "each journey is completely unique from trip to trip and person to person. I also can't really explain what it will feel like, especially since you've never done any drugs before, so there's no reference point of what it feels like to be high."

"I've been drunk?"

"Not the same thing. But, I can tell you it won't break your brain. You may feel like it is in the moment but it won't. The dosage you are taking is nowhere near enough to cause any sort of situation where you need to go to the hospital. Plus we've already ruled out any contraindications that would make you at risk of having any serious responses like a psychotic break or serotonin syndrome."

She maybe had to tell me this a dozen times. But when your OCD has caused you to spend most of your life "knowing" that you would inevitably become a psychopath, it can be hard to let in.

"My husband has taken mushrooms with his buddies and he said it feels really peaceful and he just had fun staring at the campfire for hours."

"Again, not the same thing. Recreational use is not the same as therapeutic use. You may feel peaceful, but you also may feel overwhelming fear or grief."

"How can I avoid that? That sounds like a bad trip and I do *not* want to have a bad trip."

"That's not a bad trip. A bad trip is what happens when someone takes way too much or they aren't in a safe mindset or setting which causes them to have an intensely negative experience with zero useful insight. Fear and grief are a part of healing. Sometimes your body needs to feel those feelings but your ego brain has fought to keep them quiet. That is why it is really important to work on your ability to release to your experience beforehand. You have to accept it, and yourself, no matter how it goes."

Set and setting was something I heard about from everyone once I started exploring the idea of psychedelics. Psychonauts (aka shroom fans) loved saying it. I learned that "set" means your mindset. *Am I in a good headspace? Have I set an intention for my experience?* Things like that. "Setting" is where you are during the trip. I needed to be in a safe, controlled environment with someone I trusted, where I could be the focus of the experience. I chose my hammock on the back porch and Brad was the obvious pick for my facilitator. He was made for the role, but that didn't stop me from being terrified that I would say or do something while I was tripping that would make him stop loving me.

I worked with my therapist on how to get in a good mindset, which was mostly about releasing, releasing, and more releasing. Everyone I told I was doing this, who had experience with shrooms, went on and on about my need to *release*. It was pretty annoying, actually, because the more they said it the more I worried I couldn't do it. "Just release to it", "don't resist", "let the experience be", "if you fight it, you'll get stuck in an endless negative loop". I wanted to tell all of them, "If I knew how to release to tough experiences, do you think I'd be here right now?! What do you fucking mean?!"

To practice stupid releasing, I put my arm in an ice bath so I could learn to release to discomfort/pain I knew was good for me. I got in a sensory deprivation tank to practice releasing to the sound of nothing but my own mind. I did meditations where I imagined falling into a scary hole and then landing in the safety of my own arms. I could tell it was helping, but I knew I was in control during every one of those scenarios. I could pull my arm out of the ice bath, hop out of the deprivation tank, or end a meditation whenever I wanted. I couldn't exactly stop myself from tripping on shrooms.

I still needed to set my intention. I knew it was related to the mommy issues that were triggered by Mama's cancer diagnosis but I couldn't quite pinpoint how to word what I was looking for. *Release me of my mommy issues?* Seemed a little too specific. *Give me a sense of peace?* Perhaps a little too broad.

"What feeling has your mom's cancer sparked in you that has been the most difficult to process?" my therapist asked, always gently guiding me back to the damn intention.

I thought for a moment.

"The feeling of being trapped. Like all the power is back in her hands again. I can't stop her from dying and I have to do whatever she needs while she's alive. She's not asking for anything, but I'm constantly waiting for that to change. And whatever she wants I will owe it to her and there's nothing I can do about it. She's a dying woman and all I can think about is myself. I need to just get over these mommy issues. But I can't seem to. I feel trapped in a cage with all of it."

"What would liberate you from feeling trapped?"

"To know that I am free."

Show me that I am free. There it was. My intention for my very first psilocybin experience. I needed to know that it was still possible to feel some sense of freedom even when everything felt like it was closing in around me.

"That's it." she said. "Now, remember, you are in control of your intention, but you are not in control of how the mushrooms respond to it. In fact, trying to control your trip is the opposite of releasing and would be a one-way ticket to an unpleasant experience."

I didn't miss the irony that I would have to release control in order to discover that I was free. Immediately ignoring what my therapist said, my brain started trying to create a plan for the trip. I guess I hoped my plan would somehow seep its way into my subconscious and tell the mushrooms how to do their job.

Here was my plan (that I felt was a pretty good one): *Show me that I am free by letting go of my mommy issues. I've been complaining about and blaming Mama for long enough. She hadn't done anything truly problematic in years. In reality, she hadn't really done that much to me. Most of my issues were from watching what she did to Pal. She and I hardly had any arguments. Can I really be 40 years old and complaining that I saw my mommy be mean to my sister when I was a kid? It was time to get over it already, I've milked this for long enough. The shrooms should show me that it wasn't that bad so I can release my mommy issues. That will make me feel free so I can focus on being the daughter she needs and stop obsessing over myself.*

When it was time to create my playlist to listen to during the trip, I used it as the perfect opportunity to make my suggestions a little louder. I filled it with songs about forgiveness and letting go of pain. I intentionally omitted my favorite "mommy issues song" from the playlist, *Leader of the Landslide* by The Lumineers. It's the song I would blast at full volume, sing at the top of my lungs, and sob in self pity from the first note til the last. That was definitely not the vibe I was going for here. It was time to let go of all that whining and self pity and find some compassion and forgiveness for Mama.

By the time my trip day had arrived, my biggest fear was no longer that it would be scary or go wrong. It was that it wouldn't be impactful at all. Now I had done so much preparing for a big shift that the biggest threat was not having a big shift. I was secretly worried that I might be immune to getting high. Afterall, I hadn't ever been high before so maybe I just... can't?

"One last question," I asked my therapist on our last session before my trip, "will they make me nauseous? Nausea is the worst feeling in the world to me."

"Maybe a little at first, but it always goes away after the first few minutes."

"Oh, ok, I can handle a few minutes."

The very first symptom I felt was nausea. *My therapist said this won't last long, just hang in there.* My body started to tingle. I first felt the tingling in my mouth, then in the tips of my fingers, and pretty soon

213

my whole body felt like it was vibrating slightly. I knew it was time to put on the mask and start my playlist. *Hopefully this nausea will be fading soon.*

At first, my music sounded normal, but slowly it started to change. It echoed at times and changed in tempo at other times, like someone was molding the music out of clay as it was being created. The idea creeped in my head that I had accidentally "overdosed" on the shrooms. Brad had taken a small amount of mushrooms himself to feel more "in tune" with me, so I started to also worry that maybe I had overdosed him, too. I remembered what my therapist said, "If you get worried, just release to it and remember you'll eventually come back to your normal self." I let out a sigh and prepared to face the unknown. Releasing made the nausea decrease a little. *Phew, I'm glad that's over.*

"Welp, it looks like I can, in fact, get high. I'll see you on the other side." Those were my last words to Brad before I let go and went into the other realm. I had never felt more grateful for him in my life.

I was riding in the back of a pickup truck down the interstate. It felt exhilarating but also scary. When it got a little too scary, I imagined falling into my own safe arms, like I did in the practice meditations, which felt really amazing. More amazing than I expected. It felt really good to be caught by me.

In the back of the pickup with me was Skeleton Guy. He looked like a skeleton painted for Dios de los Muertos.

"Welcome to your trip," he said, "let me show you around."

I got to feel what euphoria was like for the first time. It felt like happy if you could take it out and touch it. *I could get used to this,* I thought. Then, I started to notice how free and euphoric I was feeling. Upon noticing it I started to feel uneasy. *Is this feeling going to go away soon? Am I going to start feeling nauseous again?* As soon as the thought entered my mind, the euphoria faded away and nausea replaced it.

Along with it, a looming sense of fear hung over my head. All of the colors faded. The pickup ride no longer felt fun, now it was like I was in danger and driving towards infinite darkness. It was endless. With what little consciousness I had left, I remembered I was just a human laying in a hammock. I wanted to take off my mask, but I also remembered this was what my therapist told me I had to release to. So I accepted my nauseous fate and succumbed to the looming darkness.

Skeleton Guy tapped me on my shoulder and pointed in front of us. "Hey, it's just an overpass. The light will always return, don't worry. Welcome to your trip. This is what it will be like." We came out on the other side of the overpass and the light and euphoria returned.

Thank you, skeleton friend! I thought as I waved goodbye to him.

Skeleton Guy was right. For the next four and a half hours I cycled through feeling euphoric, noticing I felt euphoric, wondering when it would go away, it going away, feeling nauseous and hopeless, then remembering to release to the hopelessness, and beginning to feel euphoric again. Nausea and despair. Maddox playing the piano. Nausea and despair. The warmth of Brad's love. Nausea and despair. Being in awe of myself. Nausea and despair...

I was exhausted. I felt like I couldn't take much more. I was ready for it to just be over. But I knew I had to stay with the experience no matter how uncomfortable it got. So I did. My playlist ended, and I wanted to rip that mask off, but part of me knew my experience wasn't done, regardless of if I was. My Intuition took over like a DJ. I told Brad to play different songs, while having absolutely no idea as to why I was requesting them.

"Put it on my running playlist." my Intuition said, confidently.

Run playlist?! I thought, *Girl! I am tired. Is it really time for an amped up playlist like that?!*

"Fast forward until I say stop."

Oh god... what songs are on that playlist? Sign of the Times by Harry

215

Styles began playing. *That would make sense. It's a very soothing tune to close out with-*

"Skip!"

Ok... Dog Days Are Over by Florence and the Machine started playing. *That could be really empowering.*

"Skip!"

What the hell. My Way by Frank Sinatra started playing. *That sounds like a great way to wrap things up. I did it myyyy wayyyy...*

"Skip!"

Jesus Christ what is she looking for?!

And then it started playing. A song I had completely forgotten was on that playlist. A song that was only on the playlist for moments when I wanted to rage-run all my pain away. *Leader of the Landslide* by The Lumineers. The mommy issues song that I intentionally avoided putting on my trip playlist. The one song I knew I could always count on to trigger my mommy issues and rip my guts to shreds.

Skip! Skip! Hello?! Skip!

The words were stuck in my throat. Brad saw me struggling to speak and had his finger hovered over *fast forward* so he could press it the second I say go. But no words would come out.

"Fuck it." I finally said, tossing my hands in the air. *You want me to release? Let's fucking release.*

I prepared myself for total annihilation. As the melody built I feared for the worst. I imagined all the nausea returning for one last hoorah and beating me to a pulp. Instead, when the melody finally climaxed, a golden light surrounded me. It looked completely different from the visuals I had seen for the last four hours. My nausea lifted, and I somehow knew it would not be returning. I was wrapped in total peace. The cycle had ended, this was a different feeling. Neither euphoria nor fear. Just peace.

That looming feeling that you get when things are going "too" well, that feeling we've been showing you during this entire trip... Mama is where that feeling was born. It started with her. You owe her nothing. You are entitled to all of the pain you feel.

I came to this realm to find a way to heal my wounds around Mama, so I could show up for her while she was dying from cancer. And the mushrooms told me I don't owe her anything. They validated that things were as bad as my body remembered them... maybe worse.

Though not at all according to my plan, that was exactly what I needed to hear. Having the burden of obligation lifted made everything I did for her a choice. A gift of compassion. I was free to do whatever I wanted. Before, I knew I would get leery if things ever got a little "too good", but if you had asked me why I did that I would have said it was because of Daddy's unexpected death. Hands down. My trip helped me see the looming feeling was present long before that.

For days after my trip, the looming feeling continued to show up. Only it showed up as IBS issues.

"I'm not sure it's better now that I'm aware of that looming feeling." I said to my therapist in an integration session. "It feels like when someone points out a bruise you didn't know was there before, but now you can't stop poking it. My IBS has been flaring up really bad. I keep catching myself checking in with how my stomach is feeling and wondering when it's going to feel bad again. And then it starts to feel bad."

"Sometimes the mushrooms point out a pattern that needs to be addressed or replaced. When you think about your IBS, what are you saying to yourself before it starts to flare up again?"

"I'll be feeling fine. But then I'll notice that I'm feeling fine and start to wonder if something might ruin it. So I start to assess what I've recently eaten. Then I worry about whether that food might make me sick. I just keep checking in with myself until I finally do feel sick. I'm like, *'Are you feeling bad now? What about now? Now?'* It's maddening!"

"Your body is pointing out a pattern that has been existing inside you all along. This is a chance to replace the pattern. What can you replace it with? What are you *really* wanting to ask yourself when you ask 'Are you feeling sick'?"

"I guess I really just want to know if I'm feeling ok. I want to feel ok. So I guess I'm really asking *'How are you feeling?'*"

"That's it! Great! What if you replaced *'Are you starting to feel bad?'* with *'How are you feeling?'*... and could you take it a step further and have a default answer that is more positive? Like 'fine' or 'good' or..."

"Strong." *How are you feeling? Strong.* I liked that. And perhaps for the first time in my life, I believed it.

"Perfect."

When I left her office I replaced my compulsion to ask myself *"Are you feeling bad?"* with *"How are you feeling?"* and my default answer was *"Strong"*. My IBS issues dissipated. It still flared up when I was under extra stress, of course, but I went from 2-3 episodes a week to once a month. All because my brain finally let me objectively observe a pattern that was quietly happening in my subconscious every minute of every day for the majority of my life.

As grateful as I was for all of those messages and gifts, I was pretty confident I would never touch those shrooms again. Therapeutic tripping was a real kick in the ass. There was nothing recreational about them, unless you're the kind of person who enjoys hours of nausea and facing deep rooted issues head on.

Except... there was one thing I just couldn't get out of my head...

58

THE PEASANT GIRL AND THE QUEEN

The mushrooms were calling me to come back. I know how that sounds. Like a crazy shroom lady. I know because if someone would have said that to me a year ago, that's exactly what I would have called her... and then slowly backed away and looked for the nearest exit.

But there's no other way to say it than I felt called. The entire time during my first trip, "they" kept beckoning for me to stay longer. At the time I wasn't sure how to take it. Was it a gentle beckoning or like when the ghost was calling to Carolanne through the TV in *Poltergeist*? I assumed the *Poltergeist* option and it creeped me the hell out... at the time. But after my trip was over, with every passing day, I found myself wishing I had listened to "them" and stayed longer or dove deeper. Slowly, something I said I never wanted to do again, I began to miss.

I shared that feeling with my therapist and she agreed the mushrooms were "calling" me to return. And they didn't only want me to return, but to return *open*. Open to what, exactly? I had no idea.

I am open. What do you want to show me?

My intention for the 2nd trip was a lot easier to come up with than the first one. For my next experience I knew there could be no hiding or resisting. No leaving scary songs out of the playlist. No expectations for how I think it should go. No taking smaller doses (which was my original plan, to barely take any so I could hold on tight to my ego and hope the mushrooms didn't notice). I needed to go in prepared for an ass kicking.

I chose songs that punched me right in the gut. *April Come She Will* by Simon and Garfunkel, a song I listened to on repeat after Pal moved away. *No Need to Argue* by The Cranberries, a song I cried my eyes out to when Daddy died. *The Last of the Mohicans* soundtrack, a movie I escaped to over and over when I was living alone with Mama and Larry. *Like Real People Do* by Hozier, a song that reminded me of all the pain I brought with me into my marriage. *Bluebird* by Alexis Ffrench, a song Maddox could play beautifully on the piano that always reminded me of the incredible responsibility I carried by being his mother. This was no lightweight trip music, and I knew better than to try and predict the plan this time. I opened myself to any and all plans.

Down went my shroom broth, once again. No nausea this time, thank god, just tingling. Once the tinglies hit, I nestled into my cozy spot with my fur blankie, put on the mask, and started the playlist. *Come and get me, other realm.*

I was ready for anything: nausea, gut punches, euphoria, sheer terror, mind blowing magic - whatever the other realm wanted to throw my way. As I felt myself coming up (that is what the first phase of a trip is called), I started to see faint glimmers of color dancing to the music in my ears. This was it. I was ready. I let go and waited to see what the mushrooms had in store for me.

Then everything faded to black.

The lights went out, the tingly feeling vanished, the music sounded normal. All of the symptoms went away. I was just a girl, lying on a couch, listening to music.

What the hell is going on? I thought. *Hello?*

I waited, double checking to see if I really felt normal. I did.

Were my mushrooms duds? I began to wonder. *Had I not stored them properly and they lost their potency?*

I sat longer, waiting for something to happen. Nothing.

Ugh. I prepared for everything but this. What the hell. What did I do wrong? Dammit. I must've failed to grow the mushrooms right or something. I also failed to prepare for nothing. What did I expect, anyway? Some big special trip? I'm not special. The mushrooms weren't calling me back for anything. I'm nobody. Of course the other realm has nothing for me. I'm not fucking special. Not only am I not special, I'm a goddamn failure.

Disappointed and a little heartbroken, I tried to decide what to do. I had two choices. Give up and go about my day, or lay there and listen to my playlist anyway. I reached up to remove my mask, but then I paused.

No. Leave the mask on. I'm going to lay here and listen to this whole damn playlist. So what if I'm not special? I'm going to listen to her (my) unspecial playlist and have her (my) unspecial experience because you know what? She's (I'm) special to me.

B-O-O-M.

The lights came on. I launched into the most colorful, magical place my dreams couldn't have even conjured up. The music danced with the colors and I was the conductor. I not only entered the other realm, I was creating it.

I knew mushrooms could make people see colors, I knew they could bring insight, warp a person's sense of time, and allow people to see sounds. Hell, they could make you think devils, angels, and aliens were in your living room all at the same time. I had no idea they could make you feel like you weren't on mushrooms at all.

I knew after passing the initial test that I was in for a profound experience. And I was wide open for it. Just like I had promised in my intention. My "self" split into two beautiful figures: the peasant girl and The Queen.

The peasant girl laid in a fetal position on the ground, facing away from me. She wore worn clothes and she was exhausted. All I wanted was to fiercely protect her. She was the one that worked tirelessly to take care of me. I kept begging the mushrooms to please leave her alone and just let her rest. If they were going to be harsh this time, please do not be harsh to her.

The Queen was one badass bitch. She rose up out of the ground with twisted roots, thorny vines, and mossy limbs for a crown, with a radiant green light that glowed from within her heart. She had an Army of Ravens that flew around her. We all respected The Queen. She was the one who made the playlist and we were gonna listen to it. You don't fuck with The Queen.

I was somehow both of them, plus me, all at the same time.

I knew my playlist was approaching the gut-ripping intentional songs. I worried about what would happen to all of us when those songs started.

"Don't worry," said The Queen, "we're done hurting. I will carry you over those songs."

And carry me she did. When the painful songs came on, all of which I never made it through in the physical realm without sobbing, they didn't hurt at all. In fact, they sounded beautiful. I floated right over them. I felt absolutely no sadness or pain, only strength and love. It changed how I would hear those songs forever. I haven't shed a tear during any of them since (except maybe tears of gratitude and joy).

For four hours I was invincible. As I felt the effects of the mushrooms wearing off, I was devastated at the idea of having to return to the physical realm. I promised the peasant girl I would not forget her, and I promised The Queen I would remember who the fuck I was. I left the trip but I carried them both out with me.

As beautiful as that trip was, I was a walking ball of rage for at least a week after. I was pissed. The Queen had made me keenly aware of all the people who, for my entire life, benefitted from the peasant girl and never told me I was The Queen. I had walked around with an invisible debt I felt I owed to anyone who loved me. But now I saw there never was a debt to begin with. I had been carrying a lot of people's burdens and pain, and I was ready to put that shit down.

59

NACKTBADEN

"Let's go Nacktbaden!" said my German friend Katja.

I was confused and looked to the other German in the room, her best friend, to see if she could translate.

Katja and I had been friends since our children were in diapers (Katja's name has not been changed, as there is no need to protect the weird). We met at the preschool where I worked and her kids attended. Maddox was friends with her children, Lily and Paul. She was one of the mom friends that I once wasn't initially sure I belonged with, but as the years passed we both began to show our true selves to one another and realized we made much better unmasked friends than masked. Many of those other mom friends fell away as time went on, but she remained. I learned over the years that I connect well with people who are not native-born to the US. I think there is a kindredness in feeling like you're surrounded by humans you don't understand, a feeling I had always been all-too-familiar with, without explanation.

"Oh, yes. What is the English word… Nacktbaden… Hmmm…" her friend said.

I didn't know what *Nacktbaden* was but I had gathered that, whatever it was, I was about to do it.

"When you swim naked." Katja said, "What is it called?"

"*Skinny dipping?*" I asked, with a lump in my throat.

"Yes! That's it! Let's go skinny dipping!" she tapped her hands on the table and stood up in a jolt of excitement.

My stomach spun tighter and tighter, like a swing when you turn round and round until you think the chains might snap in half at any moment.

Oh, here we go again. Women getting naked with each other.

They could see from the look on my face that I was not thrilled with the translation of *Nacktbaden*.

"You have to, Cindy. Come on!" They motioned for me to get up and head to the pool with them.

I had not planned to be naked in front of my friends that evening. Nowhere on Katja's birthday invitation did it say "nudity required". Not only that, but she lived in a condominium with a shared pool. So I would not only be naked in front of a group of women I knew, but perhaps a hundred people I didn't know as well.

Not wanting to be the party pooper, I got up to follow them and, on the way to the pool, began to play out all of my fears in my head.

I am almost 40 years old and I have still never been naked in front of a friend before. I don't even like being naked in front of Brad. I feel embarrassed that this is so difficult for me. But I'm worried if I don't participate they'll judge me.

I watched from behind as the gaggle of (mostly European) women whooped and hollered in excitement as we got closer and closer to the pool. I looked at our various body shapes and how little it mattered to them.

They aren't like the other women I've been friends with before. These aren't normal women. Each one of these women are totally different and yet totally accepted. Some are opinionated, some are modest, some are quirky, some are stylish, some are nerdy, and some are downright weird. They've always shown up authentically for me and allowed space for my uniqueness. I love these women. I belong with them.

Clothes began flying the moment we hit the deck of the pool area. In the comfort of the moonlight, all shapes and sizes shed their layers with reckless abandon. While most of the women were naked almost immediately, I did notice a couple of women weren't participating. I knew that was my out. I wouldn't be the only one. That was when I realized I actually *wanted* to do it.

At first, I went to a private corner and turned the least flattering parts of my body away from their gaze and removed my clothes as modestly as possible. I folded them and put them neatly in order so I could quickly get them back on when it was time to leave. Then I made a mad dash to the pool. By the time my feet reached the water, I didn't care what angle anyone saw me at. I was liberated of self-consciousness.

The husbands stood on the balcony of the condo and whistled and cheered for their beautiful naked wives. I could finally see why women got naked together. It felt girlish and wild, yet safe and accepting. I wasn't wrong for not being able to be naked around women before, I was just trying to be naked around the wrong ones.

60

A SENSE OF URGENCY

Where is it, I thought, *where is the answer?* I frantically flipped through the pages looking for the words that I knew at one point were there. I was feeling exhausted but couldn't lay down until I solved the mystery. *I know the answers are in here somewhere, I'm just not reading carefully enough. Ugh! Why do my eyes have to bounce around the page like that?!*

My body began to feel heavier and heavier but I fought it in order to keep searching for the answer. Page after page turned, ten pages forward, six pages back. *I know it's in here.*

Finally, the sheer exhaustion began to take me over. I collapsed on the bed in total disappointment with myself. *Why can't I just figure it out? Why does it take me so long to do things? I can't spare this kind of time, this is urgent.* I hoped to drift off to sleep. But as exhausted as I was, my body couldn't rest. My eyes fixed on the ceiling as it began to rotate. A beautiful stained glass ceiling with intricate patterns and awe-inspiring colors. Each piece of glass seemed perfectly placed. *Someone made this,* I thought. *Someone figured out how to make this. I* watched as the pattern connected effortlessly. *They make it look so easy. I bet whoever made this has the answers I'm looking for.*

I lifted off the bed and floated towards the ceiling. Up, up, and then a little too far up for my taste, until my face was pressed against the glass. *The answers are here. I just have to find them.* I began to feel my way around the stained glass patterns looking for answers. *This all seems to connect but I don't understand how.* I tried to push myself off of the ceiling so I could see the picture from afar again, where it made more sense. But my body was pressed so close and something was holding me in place. *This is too close. I can't see the answers if it's too close.* Frustration set in and again I noticed my exhaustion.

I am so tired. Why can't I just rest? Every time I try to rest I am flooded with urgency. Urgency to find answers. Answers to what? I don't know but I need to find them. People are depending on me.

The song changed. The stained glass ceiling disappeared. I was relieved to feel the pressure against my face ease off. Now I was nestled inside a lush green leaf. I'm not sure if I was tiny or the leaf was giant but it felt amazing. It closely mirrored the hammock my body was laying in, in the physical realm. I felt myself drifting down a gentle stream. I realized I wasn't drifting, I was being pushed along by women. Women who wore tunics, like ancient Greek tunics. Only the fabric was made out of things found in nature; moss, leaves, etc. I was grateful for their kindness in letting me rest. Surely they knew how I had failed to find the answers and yet they weren't being cruel about it.

"Thank you for not being angry with me." I said as I lay in a fetal position on my side, finally able to rest.

"Why would we be angry with you?" they said with gentle looks of confusion on their faces, which in return confused me.

"Because I'm failing everyone. I can't find the answers and I'm so tired. Thanks for not being mean to me about that."

Their confusion intensified. "What do you mean? Of course we're not being mean to you, look at everything you are doing for us."

They motioned beyond the horizon and showed me an endless row of women waiting for their turn to pass me down the stream. They were my ancestors and they were grateful for me. I was their Breaker of Cycles.

The song changed. I wanted to celebrate being The Breaker of Cycles but my sense of urgency immediately returned. I saw men being crushed under cogs, gears, and wheels. They had built the machine but now it was crushing them. I rushed to help them but there was nothing I could do. The machine was too heavy for me to lift. All I could do was sit with them and hold their hands as they were crushed. I wanted to be there for them but I also wanted to celebrate and experience joy for what I had just learned.

"Don't leave us!" they begged.

"But I really want to celebrate. I can't help you right now anyway. I don't have the answers."

"But if you celebrate you'll forget about our pain." They squeezed tighter to my hands.

"I promise I won't forget about you. Please let me go celebrate. I promise I'll always remember you and the pain. I will think about it even as I celebrate. I will celebrate *because* of your pain, it will make me grateful for my joy." With that they let me go. Joy carried me into the sky, the pain still tucked into a pocket next to my heart, helping to propel me higher.

The song changed. I was back with my ancestors. All of them. They sang *Past Lives* by BØRNS to me, and told me they gave me everything I needed to be The Breaker of Cycles. I was enough just as I was. My ancestors and my descendants celebrated together because they all benefited from the work I was doing. They gave me that sense of urgency, but I didn't have to use it all the time. It was ok to rest too. Anything I did was more than enough. I could lay the urgency down as a burden and pick it back up again as an insurmountable strength.

I knew I was lucky to have been given that role. Many people in my

BRIGHT GIRL, LACKS FOCUS

ancestry had the role of causing pain, how fortunate was I to have the role of healing it? I left all of the rage The Queen had been carrying there. How could I be enraged when there was so much to celebrate and be grateful for?

Psychedelics created a space for my Intuition to come forward. They gave me a gift. The gift of unconditional self-love. I promised to, in return for that gift, never betray myself again.

It turned out, though, there was more to life than just loving myself. A few days after that trip, I received this text from Mama:

"Great news! Immunotherapy worked! The doctor says there are no detectable cancer cells in my body. I was told I had six months to live and now I am cancer free! Let's celebrate!"

61

MOTHER'S DAY

I had only seen Mama once during her battle with cancer, briefly at Christmas. For that visit we were given strict instructions from her ahead of time not to mention the C-word. At the time, we all thought it was the last Christmas we would have with her. And we had to pretend like it was just another year. Now, five months later, on Mother's Day of 2023, we were getting together to celebrate the fact that she was in remission.

In the car ride on the way to meet her, my brain was in a thought spiral. *Will she be her old self or the new laid back, low maintenance self we've grown accustomed to over the last year? Is she angry with us for not being more involved in her life during her battle with cancer? If so, will her anger derail all the growth I've made lately? Did she really even have cancer?* I couldn't believe I was back to that old intrusive thought again, but her extreme response to immunotherapy was rare and seemed too good to be true. I watched a lot of people die from cancer, I had never seen anyone come back from stage 4.

Then I saw her. I immediately noticed she looked different. She had lost about 40-50 pounds due to the chemo, but that wasn't it. It was something else. Her white-blonde hair looked soft, like a doll's hair.

Her porcelain skin had aged and wrinkled in a way I hadn't noticed before. I found myself strangely thinking, *She looks angelic.*

As we gave her a cliche Mother's Day flower arrangement and sat down for lunch, I searched anxiously for clues for what mood she was in. It was a familiar habit from all the times I had searched for clues as a child. The secret would usually be kept in how much she was wringing her hands, or how tightly her smile stretched across her teeth. Surprisingly, she seemed the most relaxed I had maybe ever seen her. Considering she had just survived cancer, was seeing us for the first time in months, and was in a public location (she absolutely despised going into public), this was perplexing.

"Girls, it has been quite a journey!" she opened, stating the obvious.

"I know!" said Pal, "You look so healthy. I'm so happy for you!"

"Can ya'll believe I was told I had six months to live six months ago? And look at me now! It is a true miracle that the cancer is gone and I'm alive."

"You didn't tell us that!" I said, finally chiming in after allowing everyone else to speak and reveal the tones of their voices.

"I know, I know, I didn't want to scare ya'll. I didn't want to believe it myself."

"I feel like we don't even know anything about what you've been through. Are they sure it won't come back?" Pal responded.

"Well, I will get routine scans. But even the doctor was shocked, he waited for the scans *and* the bloodwork before he actually believed it. I guess only 20% of people respond to immunotherapy as well as I did. It's good to know now in case it ever does come back."

"I can't believe you didn't tell us any of that." I said.

"I know. I didn't want to worry you girls. I really was in denial myself. I thought that if I believed what he said then it would come true. I didn't want ya'll to see me struggle, I wanted you to see me strong."

"I'm sorry you had to go through that. I hate cancer. Several of Daddy's family members have died from it lately, it's a terrible thing." Pal said.

"They have? Oh that's awful. Unfortunately, immunotherapy isn't successful for everyone like it was for me. I actually feel guilty about that. They said it's called survivor's guilt. Why should I get to live when so many other people die? Especially the Garretts. They are the most good-hearted people. I always loved them. My family *acted* like a good family. You know, they went to church every week and the kids were always dressed nice. But the Garretts really *were* a good family, the real deal. They were so genuine and loving to me always."

I had never heard her speak that way about Daddy's family. In fact, for my entire life she barely talked about Daddy at all, and if she did she certainly didn't use words like "genuine" and "loving". She usually liked to pretend like he never existed. I often wondered if she treated us the way she did because we were a painful reminder that she had ever loved him.

"Don't feel guilty," I reassured her, "you being healthy doesn't cause someone else to be sick. I'm grateful you're ok."

As the words came out of my mouth I wondered if I really meant them. I had questioned several times over the last year if her death would be a relief to me, but in that moment I truly was grateful she had survived.

"Having cancer really changed me, ya'll. I used to be afraid of everything, but now I'm not afraid of anything," she said, as she sat up straight and swung her shoulders side to side with confidence.

Her words illuminated a piece of the puzzle to her story I had never noticed before. "I used to be afraid of everything." *Huh.* I thought, *She has been afraid this whole time.* When she stopped me from seeing Little Mama and Pal after Daddy died, it was because she was afraid of them taking me away from her. When she accused Larry of looking at other women, it was out of fear that he would find someone else and leave. When she accused me of plotting against her, it was out of fear of me not loving her anymore. Fear was driving her behavior and, unfortunately, it was her behavior that made all of those fears come true.

Prior to that perspective, I found comfort in calling her a narcissist, and every therapist I saw was happy to oblige me. I thought she did those things to me because she hated me. My lack of full perspective left me with only one picture to paint of her in my mind. A picture of a woman who did mean things that she knew were mean and she did them because she cared about herself more than she cared about me. Now I could see it wasn't that simple. I was looking across the table at my mom minus the fear. She wasn't using her cancer to get pity or control like I would have predicted. She didn't think she survived because she was special, like the narcissist I imagined her to be. She was humble, guilty even, for having survived. Her fear was no longer obstructing my view from the person that she really was beneath it.

She went on to tell us about plans she had when she was 18 to leave home and work for PanAm as a flight attendant. She and her best friend had applied and been hired and everything. But the day before they left, her friend backed out to be with her boyfriend. Mama didn't think she could go through with it alone so she backed out too. I could see how fear had dictated her fate way back before I knew her.

She talked about a roommate she had, who had attempted suicide and she was the one who found her. She talked about how she met Daddy, and how hard she fell for his electric green eyes. She said he got her address from a friend and showed up at her house one night and insisted she go on a date with him. In one hour I learned more about Mama than I had in my lifetime prior.

We left with a sincere hug and a light feeling in my chest that I wasn't used to feeling after spending time with Mama. Pal and I rode back home together with none of the venting and note comparing we typically had to do.

In the days following, memories of her resurfaced that I had suppressed. Good memories. Her cuddling with me at bedtime and singing *The Mockingbird Song*. How much she loved baking with me and making homemade playdough. Singing Creedence Clearwater Revival at the tops of our lungs in the car. Having inside jokes and using funny accents with one another that we made up. I realized I really did miss her sometimes. I missed the days when her mood was stable and fear hadn't triggered her. I did love her. It was just complicated for both me and her.

She had coped with her trauma and pain by letting fear control her whole world. It kept her safe, but it pushed everyone else away. It didn't excuse the harm she caused and it didn't make her immune from ever causing harm again. But it helped me see her as human. A human not that different from me, actually. I've hurt people out of my own fear. I've retreated into my Inside World and away from others. It didn't look the same but only because I had her to show me how much it would hurt if I did what she did. I came home from Mother's Day with a much better gift than the flowers I gave her. I came home without mommy issues.

62

INVENTING CHILDHOOD

By my 41st birthday, I really felt like I had moved mountains. When I looked back over my life, it seemed like a thousand lifetimes. I was unrecognizable from that girl sobbing on that shitty brown couch and at the same time she was right by my heart. Better than giving Maddox the childhood I never had, I managed to give myself the childhood I never had so that he could just have whatever childhood he needed.

The most surprising thing about healing was I didn't feel it in the big moments, like I imagined I would. I thought healing meant birthdays wouldn't remind me of the countdown of how many years were left until I'm the same age Daddy was. The big moments still had a little stain of grief to them. But I was able to allow that grief to be there without growing into even bigger grief over the fact that I'm still a little sad on birthdays. I felt healing in the small spaces in between big moments. It's amazing how many of those moments there are. In the car rides with perfectly timed songs, a hilariously inappropriate joke Maddox felt safe enough to tell, in the time I spent teaching myself how to make a perfect cup of tea, or in closed eyes and a face turned towards the sun while on a hike. That is where real healing was present. In the subtle spaces between.

I wanted to express gratitude that all of this was even possible. I felt grateful for the mushrooms, my ancestors who showed up to guide me, Daddy who was my beacon to follow, all of the researchers and scientists who helped me understand how my body works, and all the friends and family who held space while I figured myself out. And surprisingly, I now felt grateful for Mama for the first time in my life. And not the "I'm glad she sucked because it toughened me up" kind of grateful, but *authentic* gratitude. I truly saw she was doing her best just like I was. I had compassion for why she became who she was and I was grateful she played the villain for so many years so I would have something to overcome and grow from. I needed permission to set myself free from the curses she carried from the generations before her. I'm pretty sure cancer finally set her free too but I never would have been able to recognize it if I was not free myself. It felt like we were meeting on the other side of a battle, tattered and torn, but knowing we both won. And forgiving each other for the things we had to do to make it to the other side.

The best way I could think to celebrate and express gratitude for it all was to go back to the other realm and tell them all myself. I took shrooms one more time on my 41st birthday. I couldn't wait to spread my gratitude around.

The song *Thank You* by Alanis Morissette came on. That was my chance.

"Thank -"

"Not now!"

The Daughters of Quiet Minds by Stars Of The Lid came on, a very meditative song that relates to breaking generational cycles.

"Thank youuu?" my words echoed into a void and landed with a thud into a vast black hole.

Like passing strangers as I begged for change, no one was interested in helping a sista out by accepting my gratitude.

"It's not time yet," and "Wait your turn," were the closest to a response I got, and they were said with hurried irritation.

I kept circling back to try to say thank you and kept being interrupted. It felt rude and I was beginning to wonder why I the hell wanted to thank them in the first place. The music even felt like it was interrupting me, blocking me from what I had to say. Like the artists were speaking for me, but getting it all wrong.

I have something to say, dammit! Why aren't you listening?! I'm trying to thank you! Accept my fucking gratitude!

The song changed to *Helvegen* by Wardruna. Their music is not for the faint of heart. It's all intense drum beats and deep, masculine chanting. To combine them with shrooms takes some balls. Lucky for me, I now had a heavy set of them. As is common with psychedelic trips, with the song change came a complete change in tone.

I was in an old Viking village. I was a little girl covered in mud. Much like the peasant girl, I was in worn clothing, barefoot, and easily overlooked. I heard a crow overhead, it signaled that The Summoner was coming. The sound of the crow struck fear in many hearts and hope in others. When I heard him, my eyes widened with intrigue.

Oh, shit. I thought, *someone is in trouble. I've gotta see this.*

A crowd of people began to rush past me to go watch for the arrival of The Summoner, while other people ran in the opposite direction, afraid of its wrath. I was lost and confused in the chaos but I knew I wanted to see The Summoner. But the crowd was growing massive and dense.

I tried to climb over their shoulders or on nearby objects so I could get a better view. I knew The Summoner would be here soon and I wanted to witness the moment of arrival. But I couldn't see a thing. Just backs and shoulders blocking my way and above that a darkening sky. Thunder rolled in and the crows got more excited. Rain poured and I began slipping in the mud, losing even more traction and hope at ever seeing what the crowd was staring at. I made one final attempt to jump up to see and a loud crack of lightning struck down. My eyes went white. I had been Summoned.

I stood on stage. My massive body was shaped like a devil, but not evil. I held a hammer in my hand and listened to the chants and drums as they awakened me. I was The Summoner. I looked at the strength in my hands and shook with both extreme power and complete overwhelm. I was here to Summon my army.

What army? I wondered.

But The Summoner already knew the answer to that question. His chants were in Nordic but I felt I knew exactly what they meant.

The Summoner: I am here for all of the wildflowers. The misunderstood children who are easily broken by the world. We are criticized for our brokenness by the people who shattered us. We try so hard to hold our broken pieces close so as not to hurt anyone else, often cutting ourselves instead. I am here to tell them they are not just broken. They are also light and warmth and people use them for that warmth. They suffocate us and we contort ourselves to reach for some space to breathe. We try to follow their rules so that we might have some peace and time to ourselves. But they never say it's good enough. They never thank us for the warmth. Instead, they say we are too distracted, too intense, too strange... too much. But we aren't too much. We are so much. They tell us we are weeds. But they never tell us how weeds adapt. Or how they are also wildflowers.

I have been given a short time on this planet to find the wildflowers and tell them that they are wildflowers. I feel that sense of urgency with every waking moment of my life. Whether I'm speaking to my clients, my son, or a person I just met in line at a coffee shop who felt compelled to talk to me about their pain. I am always walking and speaking with a sense of urgency to set them all free. I was given the gift of a sense of urgency from my trauma and the trauma of generations before me. I'm not going to take it for granted. When I was a child I used my gift to comfort Mama so that I may have a moment's comfort. As a teen and young adult I used my gift to manipulate others so that they would meet my needs when I didn't think I could meet my own. Now, as an adult, I have released shame so my gift no longer behaves as a curse. I can now use my gift too tell others that they are not the failure/monster/mistake the world tells them they are. They are pure wild magic.

I was overwhelmed with this realization and the gratitude I felt for the role I'd been given in this life. As I felt myself coming out of the trip, I looked to the mushrooms one last time to say *thank you.*

No response. A whisper beyond the music spoke softly to me. *Turn off the music.*

I released to my orders and sat in silence, unsure that I would be able to take anything away from it without the music to support me.

"Why won't you let me thank you?" I asked.

"Thank yourself. You did all of this from scratch."

I felt myself resist that message. "I appreciate that but I had help. I had inspiration and examples and guidance."

"We said, *from scratch.*"

I was almost offended at this insistence. "What about Daddy? Are you really going to argue that he didn't play a massive role in shaping me? He was the best man I have ever known to walk this earth. He's the gold standard I've held myself to all these years. I'd be content being half the person he was."

"You invented him."

"Excuse me?" I began to fear that I had gone too far with this whole self-love thing. There was no way I had invented Daddy.

"You invented him. You made him what you needed him to be, you don't see him for who he actually was."

Just as I saw Mama as human on Mother's Day, I was suddenly able to see Daddy as human as well. Yes, he was silly and fun and loving and kind. But he was also tough and imperfect and could be judgemental and intimidating. He adored me, but I only knew him until I was 13. He never saw flawed, adolescent, unlovable me. I filled in the gaps of his absence with the very best benefit of the doubt I could muster. With this veil lifted, I knew he likely would have also rejected and shamed me. I hid my grades from him because he got angry with anything less than an A. When we said goodbye to him in the hospital, Pal and I promised to make "lots of 100 A+s" in order to make him proud. He would have been horrified at the terrible grades I had my entire life.

He didn't have the patience that I invented him to have. He often lost his temper with me when I rambled on too long or couldn't remember two-step instructions.

I wasn't even sure the dinosaur pants story from Kindergarten was true. He rarely picked me up from school and if he did it would be at carpool, so I doubt my teacher ever told him how I distracted the kids by not following directions. If she had, there was a good chance he *would* have gotten onto me regardless of how fucking dumb the reason was. Because he was human, and humans have flaws.

I created an idealized version of him so that I would have something to hold on to. I created the father I needed. I concocted an amalgam of him from different versions of Robin Williams in *Mrs. Doubtfire*, *Good Will Hunting*, and *Hook* (I was obsessed with Robin growing up and Daddy looked a lot like him). They weren't as much lies as they were wishes. I invented a perfect, fictional Daddy so that I could invent my beautiful, very real life.

Realizing parts of Daddy was a thing of my own creation, I knew it was time to stop giving credit to everyone else. I was steady enough on my own feet now. I gave credit to Daddy for inspiring me. I gave credit to my mentors for my wisdom. I gave credit to researchers and scientists for my insights. I gave credit to Brad for saving me. And I gave credit to Maddox for making me a good mother. At the end of the day I had to reach for all of those things. I had to conjure them and make them real. It was time to give myself credit for the life I'd built... *from scratch.*

63

THE END

"How have you been feeling since your birthday shroom trip?" Brad asked me one lazy Sunday morning over coffee and tea.

"It's been crazy. It's really hard to describe."

"I bet. Those shrooms are no joke."

"You ain't never lied. One thing I took away for sure is I am really going to try to use my voice more and take credit for my ideas more. Like, I think I might even write a book."

"I think that's a great idea. You've been talking about it for, what, 20 years now? Now that you aren't giving away all the credit to someone else, maybe you'll actually be able to do it."

"Yeah, I feel like imposter syndrome was always in the way before, but I don't think that's as much of a problem now. I used to think I was insane for thinking I could be an author. Remember back when I lived in that shitty furnished apartment in Barnesville? That was a ridiculous thought at the time. I think sometimes I can *feel* a truth long before it makes any sense at all for it to happen."

"I never thought it was that insane. Just maybe you weren't ready yet. But I always believed you could."

"Why *did* you always believe in me, even when I seemed batshit crazy?"

"Even when you were crazy... and you *were* crazy sometimes... but even when you were, you were right. Your delivery and intensity could be too much and your timing was usually terrible but your message was never wrong. I always admired that about you."

"Really? Awww... thank you for that. I love you."

"I love you too."

Brad got up to put his coffee cup in the sink and started to walk outside to check the garden. I still sat, as usual taking forever to drink my tea, thinking.

"It's strange," I said just before he walked out the door, "There's this feeling I can't quite put my finger on but it's really intense. I feel like my mommy *and* my daddy issues are just gone. But there's this feeling in place of them that I've never felt before. It's like my brain is experiencing a new sensation but I don't know how to describe it."

"That *does* sound intense. Is it a good or a bad feeling?"

"It's hard to describe... I wish I could put you in my head so you could see what I'm talking about. It's like... empty... but not in a bad way. It's like a good kind of empty."

Brad headed outside again, shaking his head, as usual not having any idea what the hell I was talking about.

I gasped. "Oh my god-"

"What?!" he said, jerking his head back to look at me.

"Quiet. The feeling is quiet. My mind is... *quiet.*"

About the Author

Cindy Robinson is a Researcher, Author, and Neurodivergent Life Coach, who specializes in supporting humans through the neurodivergent unmasking process. Her research in neurodivergent brains and behavior shape the foundation of her practice, her books, and her life. She aims to empower people by connecting them with their own intuition by any means necessary. She is diagnosed with ASD, ADHD, and OCD, which fuels her passion to help liberate people with similar-working brains.

When she is not working to liberate neurodivergent humans, Cindy is enjoying time with her husband, Brad, whom she describes as her own personal Nick Offerman. Together they created a son, Maddox, who's inspiring soul is infinitely worth tireless efforts to break generational cycles. She is grateful daily for their endless love, support, and acceptance.

You can connect with me on:

- https://www.cindyrobinsonllc.com
- https://www.instagram.com/CINDYROBINSONLLC

Made in United States
Cleveland, OH
18 November 2024

10744866R00150